The
Almost
Christian
Discovered

or

The False Professor Tried and Cast

by

Matthew Mead

Foreword by Dr. John MacArthur

Edited by Dr. Don Kistler

Soli Deo Gloria Publications

...for instruction in righteousness...

Soli Deo Gloria Publications

A division of Soli Deo Gloria Ministries, Inc.

P.O. Box 451, Morgan, PA 15064

(412) 221-1901/FAX 221-1902

www.SDGbooks.com

*

*

ISBN 1-877611-72-7

Contents

Contents

Foreword

by John MacArthur

The Almost Christian Discovered is a rare treasure. It reveals the force and fervor of Puritan spirituality as vividly as any work I know. It delivers the kind of potent message one longs to hear, but almost never does, in this age of cheap grace and shallow conversion.

If you just happened to pick up this copy, you might be tempted to write the book off as an anachronism. You'll detect more than a hint of King Jamesian dialect. The vocabulary is classic Puritanism. Even the expression "The Almost Christian" sounds a little quaint. No wonder. We live in a day when much of what passes as evangelical preaching actually fosters superficiality.

But hold on to this book. If its language seems dated, its message is not. Matthew Mead's challenge to spurious believers is as timely as when he wrote it in 1661. More than just a period piece, this volume offers a much-needed antidote to the shallowness and flippancy that characterizes today's Christianity. It contrasts sharply with the modern tendency to embrace as a brother or sister in the faith everyone who names the name of Christ. It sounds an alarm that few today would dare even whisper.

In fact, *The Almost Christian Discovered* provides sobering proof of how far the contemporary church has slipped from the moorings of her heritage. Twentieth-century Christians, conditioned to accept carnality, worldliness, and compromise as part of the normal Christian experience, are certain to be shocked by Mead's admonition. We are not used to hearing truth presented in such straightforward and confrontive terms. Matthew Mead is no diplomat. He is a real preacher, and he speaks with prophetic accuracy.

A word of caution: this is not balm for the emotions; it is food for the soul. Those looking for a tranquilizing devotional study will not be soothed by this book. People who have come to Christ only for what they can get out of Him will find no encouragement here. On the other hand, true believers who want to deepen their walk – even struggling Christians who are open to reproof and instruction – will find plenty of sustenance on these pages.

I found in Matthew Mead a kindred spirit. Though he ministered more than 300 years ago, I feel as if I know him. I understand the passions that drove him; they're my passions too. I share his frustration over people who profess to know Christ but are indifferent or lackadaisical about spiritual matters (cf. Titus 1:16). I sense his zeal for the truth, tempered only by fear borne out of the knowledge that these are issues of eternal importance and someone might misunderstand.

To make sure no one would be confused, Mead chose a unique form of presentation. Like a lawyer arguing his case, he puts the "almost Christian" on trial. Point by point, with the clarity and precision of a first-rate prosecuting attorney, Mead exposes the guilt of those who give lip service to Christ but do not obey Him. His arguments are devastating and, in the end, the verdict is clear. The "almost Christian" is convicted.

So, by the way, are the rest of us. Everyone but the most cold-hearted reader will sense some degree of conviction. The case Mead presents is meticulous. His expose of the "almost Christian" rips the cover away from subtle forms of hypocrisy that lurk in all our hearts.

Mead realized weak and struggling Christians would read his words and ask, like the innocent disciples in the Upper Room, "Is it I?" One of his apparent fears was that some fragile believer might be hurt or discouraged by his indictment. "The gospel does not speak these things to wound believers," he wrote, "but to awaken sinners and formal professors." He acknowledged the severity of his theme, confessing a certain apprehension. He did not want it to "break the bruised reed, nor to quench the smoking flax."

Yet his greater fear was that some false Christian might take solace in the promises and comforts of the gospel. Given the choice between consoling a quasi-believer and unsettling someone who is weak in the faith, Mead believed the latter was preferable. He understood the value of self-examination, an exercise modern psycho-evangelicals seem determined to do away with.

Self-examination is thoroughly biblical. The Apostle Paul wrote, "Test yourselves to see if you are in the faith; examine yourselves! Or do you not recognize this about yourselves, that Jesus Christ is in you–unless indeed you fail the test?" (2 Corinthians 13:5).

That is exactly what this book is all about. Don't read it unless you are willing to undergo the most intense kind of spiritual inventory.

If you do read it, however, read it prayerfully and conscientiously. You're in for the most constructive spiritual pilgrimage any book can guide you through.

To The Congregation

To the congregation at St. Sepulchre's, who were the hearers at these sermons: grace and peace be multiplied:

Beloved, what the meaning of that providence was that called me to the occupation of my talent among you this summer will be best read and understood by the effects of it upon your own souls. The kindly increase of grace and holiness in heart and life can only prove it to have been in mercy. Where this is not the fruit of the Word, there it becomes a judgment. The Word travels with life or death, salvation or damnation, and brings forth one or the other in every soul that hears it. I would not for a world (were it in my power to make the choice) that my labors, which were meant and designed for the promotion of your immortal souls to the glory of the other world in a present pursuance of the things of your peace, should be found to have been a ministration of death and condemnation in the great day of Jesus Christ. Yet this, the Lord knows, is the too-common effect of the most plain and powerful preaching of the gospel. "The waters of the sanctuary" do not always heal where they come, for there are "miry and marshy places that shall be given to salt." The same word is elsewhere is Scripture rendered "barrenness"; He "turneth a fruitful land into barrenness" so that the judgment denounced upon these miry and marshy places is that the curse of barrenness shall rest upon them, notwithstanding the "waters of the sanctuary overflow them."

It is said with certainty that the gospel inflicts a death of its own as well as the law; or else how are those trees in Jude said to be "twice dead, and plucked up by the roots?" Yea, that which in itself is the greatest mercy, through the interposition of men's lusts and the efficacy of this cursed sin of unbelief, turns to the greatest judgment, as the richest and most generous wine makes the sharpest vinegar. Our Lord Christ Himself, the choicest mercy with which the bowels of God could bless a perishing world, whose coming, Himself bearing witness, was on no less an errand than that of eternal life and blessedness to the lost and cursed sons of Adam; yet to how many was He "a stone of stumbling, and a rock of offence"; yea, "a gin, and a snare", and that to both the houses of Israel, the only professing people of God at that day in the world! And is He not a stone of stumbling in the ministry of the gospel to many professors to this very day, upon which they fall and are broken? When He said, "Blessed is he whosoever shall not be offended in Me," He therein plainly supposes that, both in His person and doctrine, the generality of men would be offended in Him.

Not that this is the design of Christ and the gospel, but it comes so to pass through the corruptions of the hearts of men, whereby they make light of Christ and stand out against that life and grace which the Lord Jesus, by His blood, so dearly purchased and is, by the preaching of the gospel, so freely tendered; the wilful refusal whereof will as surely double our damnation as the acceptance thereof will secure our eternal salvation.

Oh, consider, it is a thing of the most serious concern in the world how we carry ourselves under the gospel, and with what dispositions and affections of heart soul-seasons of grace are entertained; this being taken into the consideration to give it weight, that we are the nearer to heaven or hell, to salvation or damnation, by every ordinance we sit under. Boast not, therefore, of privileges enjoyed, with neglect of the important duties thereby required. Remember Capernaum's case and tremble. As many go to heaven by the very gates of hell, so more go to hell by the gates of heaven, in that the number of those that profess Christ is greater than the number of those that truly close with Christ.

Beloved, I know the preaching of the gospel has proselytized many of you into a profession; but I fear that but few of you are brought by it to a true close with the Lord Christ for salvation. I beseech you, bear with my jealousy, for it is the fruit of a tender love for your precious souls. Most men are good Christians in the verdict of their own opinion, but you know the law allows no man to be a witness in his own case, because their affection usually overreaches conscience and self-love deceives truth for its own interest.

The heart of man is the greatest impostor and cheat in the world. God Himself states it, "The heart is deceitful above all things." Some of the deceits thereof you will find discovered in this treatise, which shows you that every grace has its counterfeit, and that the highest profession may be where true conversion is not.

The design of it is not to break the bruised reed, nor to quench the smoking flax; not to discourage the

weakest believer, but to awaken formal professors. I
would not sadden the hearts of any whom God would
not have made sad; though I know it is hard to expose
the dangerous state and condition of a professing hypocrite, but that the weak Christian will think himself
concerned in the discovery. And, therefore, as I
preached a sermon on sincerity among you for the
support and encouragement of such, so I purposed to
have printed it with this. But who can be master of his
own purposes? That is I am under such daily variety of
providences, your kindly acceptance of this will make
me a debtor for that.

The dedication hereof belongs to you on a double
account; for as it had not been preached but that love
to your souls caused it, so it had much less been
printed but that your importunate desire procured it.
And, therefore, whatever entertainment it finds in the
world, yet I hope I may expect you will welcome it, especially considering it was born under your roof and,
therefore, hopes to find favor in your eyes and room in
your hearts.

Accept it, I beseech you, as a public acknowledg-
ment of the engagements which your great and, I think
I may say, unparalleled respects have laid me under,
which I can no way compensate but by my prayers; and,
if you will take them for satisfaction, I promise to be
your remembrancer at the throne of grace, while I am,

Matthew Mead

To the Reader

Reader, I know how customary it is for men to ascend the public stage with premised apologies for the weakness and unworthiness of their labors, which is an argument that their desires (either for the sake of others' profit, or their own credit, or both) are stretched beyond the bounds of their abilities and that they covet to commend themselves to the world's censure in a better dress than common infirmity will allow. For my own part, I may truly say with Gideon, "Behold, my thousand is the meanest," my talent is the smallest, "and I am the least in my father's house"; and, therefore, this appearance in public is not the fruit of my own choice, which would rather have been on some other subject wherein I stand, in some sense, indebted to the world, or else somewhat more digested and, possibly, better fitted for common acceptation. But this is but to consult the interest of a man's own name which, in matters of this concern, is no better than a "sowing to the flesh", and the harvest of such a seed-time will be "in corruption."

You have here one of the saddest considerations imaginable presented to you, and that is how far it is possible a man may go in a profession of religion and yet, after all, fall short of salvation; how far he may run and yet not so run as to obtain. This, I say, is sad, but not so sad as true; for our Lord Christ plainly attests it: "Strive to enter in at the strait gate: for many, I say unto you, will seek to enter in, and shall not be able."

My design herein is that the formal, sleepy professor may be awakened and the close hypocrite discovered. But my fear is that weak believers may be hereby discouraged. It is hard to show how low a child of God may fall into sin and yet have true grace without the sinner being apt, thereupon, to presume. And it is just as hard to show how high a hypocrite may rise in a profession and yet have no grace without the believer being apt, thereupon, to despond. I have carefully endeavored to prevent this by showing that, though a man may go thus far and yet be but almost a Christian, yet a man may fall short of this and be a true Christian notwithstanding. Judge not, therefore, your state by any one character of a false professor you find laid down, but read the whole and then make a judgment; for I have been as careful not to give children's bread to dogs as not to use the dog's whip to scare the children.

Yet I could wish that this book might fall into the hands of such only whom it chiefly concerns, who have a name to live and yet are dead, being busy with the form of godliness but are strangers to the power of it. These are the proper subjects of this treatise, and may the Lord follow it with His blessing wherever it comes, that it may be an awakening word to all and, especially, to that generation of profligate professors with which this age abounds; who, if they keep to their church, bow the knee, talk over a few prayers and, at a good time, receive the sacrament think they do enough for heaven and, hereupon, judge their condition safe and their salvation sure, though there is a hell of sin in their hearts and the poison of asps under their lips; their minds being as yet carnal and unconverted and

their conversations filthy and unsanctified. If eternal
life is of so easy attainment, and to be had at so cheap
a rate, why did our Lord Christ tell us, "Strait is the
gate and narrow is the way which leadeth unto life, and
few there be that find it?" And why should the apostle
perplex us with such a needless injunction to give diligence to make our calling and election sure? Certainly,
therefore, it is no such easy thing to be saved, as many
make it, and that you will see plainly in the following
discourse.

FIVE IMPORTANT DUTIES

I have been somewhat short in the application of it
and, therefore, let me give you five important duties:
1. *Take heed of resting in a form of godliness, as if duties*
ex opere operato *could confer grace.* A lifeless formality
is advanced to a very high esteem in the world, as a
"cab of dove's dung" was sold in the famine of Samaria
at a very dear rate. Alas! The profession of godliness is
but a sandy foundation to build the hope of an
immortal soul upon for eternity. Remember, the Lord
Jesus Christ called him a foolish builder who founded
his house upon the sand, and the sad event proved
him so, "for it fell, and great was the fall of it." Oh,
therefore, lay your foundation by faith upon the rock
Christ Jesus; look to Christ through all and rest upon
Christ in all.
2. *Labor to see an excellency in the power of godliness, a*
beauty in the life of Christ. If the means of grace have a
loveliness in them, surely grace itself has much more;
for the goodness of the means lies in its suitableness

and serviceableness to the end. The form of godliness has no goodness in it any further than its steads and becomes useful to the soul in the power and practice of godliness. The life of holiness is the only excellent life; it is the life of saints and angels in heaven; yea, it is the life of God in Himself. As it is a great proof of the baseness and filthiness of sin that sinners seek to cover it, so it is a great proof the excellence of godliness that so many pretend to it. The very hypocrite's fair profession pleads the cause of religion, although the hypocrite is then really worst when he is seemingly best.

3. *Look upon things to come as the greatest realities;* for things that are not believed work no more upon the affections than if they had no being, and this is the grand reason why the generality of men suffer their affections to go after the world, setting the creature in the place of God in their hearts.

Most men judge the reality of things by their visibility and proximity to sense; and, therefore, the choice of that wretched Cardinal becomes their option who would not leave his part in Paris for his part in Paradise. Surely, whatever his interest might be in the former, he had little enough in the latter. Well may covetousness be called idolatry when it thus chooses the world for its god.

Oh, consider that eternity is no dream! Hell and the worm that never dies is no melancholy conceit! Heaven is no feigned Elysium! There is the greatest reality imaginable in these things. Though they are spiritual and out of the view of sense, yet they are real and within the view of faith. "Look not, therefore, at the things which are seen, but look at the things which are not seen; for the things that are seen are temporal, but the things which are not seen are eternal."

4. *Set a high rate upon your soul. What we lightly prize, we easily part with.* Many men sell their souls at the rate of profane Esau's birth-right, "for a morsel of meat"; nay, "for that which," in the sense of the Holy Ghost, "is not bread." Oh, consider your soul is the most precious and invaluable jewel in the world! It is the most beautiful piece of God's workmanship in the whole creation! It is that which bears the image of God and which was bought with the blood of the Son of God, and shall we not set a value upon it and count it precious?

The apostle Peter speaks of three very precious things:

1. A Precious Christ
2. Precious Promises
3. Precious Faith

Now, the preciousness of all these lies in their usefulness to the soul. Christ is precious, being the Redeemer of precious souls. The Promises are precious, as making over this precious Christ to precious souls. Faith is precious, as bringing a precious soul to close with a precious Christ as He is held forth in the precious promises. O take heed that you are not found overvaluing other things and undervaluing your soul. Shall your flesh, nay your beast, be loved, and shall your soul be slighted? Will you clothe and pamper your body and yet take no care of your soul? This is as if a man should feed his dog and starve his child. "Meats for the belly, and the belly for meats; but God will destroy both it and them." O let not a tottering, perishing carcass have all your time and care, as if the life and salvation of your soul were not worth the while.

5. *Last, meditate much on the strictness and suddenness of that judgment-day through which you and I must pass into an everlasting state;* wherein God, the impartial judge, will require an account at our hands of all our talents and entrustments. We must then account for time, how we have spent that; for estate, how we have employed that; for strength, how we have laid out that; for afflictions and mercies, how they have been improved; for the relations we stood in here, how they have been discharged; and for seasons and means of grace, how they have been husbanded. And look, how we have sowed here, we shall reap hereafter.

Reader, these are things that, of all others, deserve most of, and call loudest for, our utmost care and endeavors, though they are, by most, least-minded. To consider what a spirit of atheism (if we may judge the tree by the fruits and the principle by the practice) the hearts of most men are filled with who live as if God were not to be served, nor Christ to be sought, nor lust to be mortified, nor self to be denied, nor the Scripture to be believed, nor the judgment-day to be minded, nor hell to be feared, nor heaven to be desired, nor the soul to be valued, but give up themselves to a worse than brutish sensuality, "to work all uncleanness with greediness," living without God in the world! This is a meditation fit enough to break our hearts, if at least we were of holy David's temper who beheld the transgressors and was grieved, and had rivers of waters running down his eyes because men kept not God's laws.

The prevention and correction of this soul-destroying distemper is not the least design of this treatise now put into your hand. Though the chief virtue of this receipt lies in its sovereign use to assuage and cure the swelling tympany of hypocrisy, yet it may serve also, with God's blessing, as a plaster for the plague-sore of profaneness, if timely applied by serious meditation and carefully kept on by constant prayer.

Reader, expect nothing of curiosity or quaintness, for then I will deceive you; but, if you would have a touchstone for the trial of your state, possibly this may serve you. If you are either a stranger to a profession, or a hypocrite under a profession, then read and tremble; for you are the man here pointed at.

But if the kingdom of God is come with power into your soul, if Christ is formed in you, if your heart is upright and sincere with God, then read and rejoice.

I fear I have transgressed the bounds of an epistle. The mighty God, whose prerogative it is to teach to profit, whether by the tongue or the pen, by speaking or writing, bless this tract that it may be to you as a cloud of rain to the dry ground, dropping fatness to your soul; so that your fleece, being watered with the dew of heaven, you may "grow in grace, and in the knowledge of our Lord and Saviour Jesus Christ," in whom I am your friend and servant,

Matthew Mead
London
October, 1661

THE ALMOST CHRISTIAN DISCOVERED

"Almost thou persuadest me to be a Christian."
Acts 26:28

INTRODUCTION

In this chapter, you have the apostle Paul's apology and defensive plea which he makes for himself against these blind Jews who so maliciously persecuted him before Agrippa, Festus, Bernice, and the Council. In this plea, he chiefly insists upon three things:
1. The manner of his life before conversion.
2. The manner of his conversion.
3. The manner of his life after conversion.

How he lived before conversion he tells you in verses 4-13. How God wrought on him to conversion, he tells you, verses 13-18. How he lived after conversion he tells you in verses 19-23. Before conversion, he was very pharisaical. The manner of his conversion was very wonderful. The fruit of his conversion was very remarkable.

1

Before conversion, he persecuted the gospel which others preached; after conversion, he preached the gospel which he himself had persecuted.

While he was a persecutor of the gospel, the Jews loved him; but now that, by the grace of God, he had become a preacher of the gospel, the Jews hated him and sought to kill him.

He was once against Christ, and then many were for him; but now that he was for Christ, all were against him. His being an enemy to Jesus made others his friends; but, when he came to own Jesus, then they became his enemies. And this was the great charge they had against him, that, of a great opposer, he had become a great professor. Because God had changed him, therefore, this enraged them; as if they would be the worse because God had made him better. God had wrought on him by grace and they seem to envy him the grace of God. He preached no treason, nor sowed sedition; he only preached repentance, faith in Christ, and the resurrection; and, for this, he was "called in question."

This is the breviate and sum of Paul's defense and plea for himself which you find, in the sequel of the chapter, had a different effect upon his judges.

Festus seems to censure him, verse 24. Agrippa seems to be convinced by him, verse 28. The whole bench seems to acquit him, verses 30-31. Festus thinks Paul was beside himself. Agrippa is almost persuaded to be such a one as himself.

Festus thinks him mad because he did not understand the doctrine of Christ and the resurrection, "Much learning hath made thee mad." Agrippa is so affected with his plea that he is almost wrought into his principle. Paul pleads so effectually for his religion that Agrippa seems to be upon the turning point to his profession, "Then Agrippa said to Paul, Almost thou persuadest me to be a Christian."

"Almost." The words make for some debate among the learned. I shall not trouble you with the various hints upon them by Valla, Simplicius, Beza, Erasmus, and others. I take the words as we read them, and they show what an efficacy Paul's doctrine had upon Agrippa's conscience. Though he would not be converted, yet he could not but be convinced; his conscience was touched, though his heart was not renewed.

OBSERVATION. There is that in religion which carries its own evidence along with it even to the consciences of ungodly men.

"Thou persuadest me." The word is from the Hebrew, and it signifies both *suadere* and *persuadere;* either to use arguments to prevail or to prevail by the arguments used. Now, it is to be taken in the latter sense here to show the influence of Paul's argument upon Agrippa, which had almost proselyted him to the profession of Christianity. "Almost thou persuadest me to be a Christian."

"A Christian." I hope I need not tell you what a Christian is, though I am persuaded there are many who are called Christians who do not know what a Christian is; or, if they do, yet they do not know what it is to be a Christian. A Christian is a disciple of Jesus Christ, one who believes in and follows Christ. As one who embraces the doctrine of Arminius is called an Arminian, and he who owns the doctrine and way of Luther is called a Lutheran, so he who embraces, owns, and follows the doctrine of Jesus Christ is called a Christian.

The word is taken more largely and more strictly: more largely, and so all who profess Christ come in the flesh are called Christians in opposition to heathens who do not know Christ; and to the poor blind Jews who will not own Christ; and to the Mahometan who prefers Mahomet above Christ. But now, in Scripture, the word is of a more strict and narrow acceptation. It is used only to denominate the true disciples and followers of Christ. "The disciples were first called Christians at Antioch. If any man suffer as a Christian, let him not be ashamed"; who is, as a member and disciple of Christ; and so in the text, "Almost thou persuadest me to be a Christian."

The word is used only in these three places in all the New Testament and, in each of them, it is used in the sense aforementioned.

The Italians make the name to be a name of reproach among them and, usually, abuse the word Christian to signify a fool. But if, as the apostle said, the preaching of Christ is to the world foolishness, then it is no wonder who the disciples of Christ are, to the world, fools. Yet it is true, in a sound sense, who they are, for the whole of godliness is a mystery. A man must die who would live; he must be empty who would be full; he must be lost who would be found; he must have nothing who would have all things; he must be blind who would have illumination; he must be condemned who would have redemption; so he must be a fool who would be a Christian. "If any man among you seem to be wise, let him become a fool, who he may be wise." He is the true Christian who is the world's fool but wise to salvation.

Thus you have the sense and meaning of the words briefly explained. The text needs no division, and yet it is a pity the word "almost" should not be divided from the word "Christian." It is of little avail, however, to divide them as they are linked in the text, unless I could divide them as they are united in your hearts. This would be a blessed division if the "almost" might be taken from the "Christian," that you may not be only *propemodum* but *admodum;* not only *almost* but *altogether* Christians. This is God's work to effect it, but it is our duty to persuade to it. Oh, that God would help me to manage this subject so that you may say, in the conclusion, "You persuade me not almost, but altogether, to be a Christian!" The observation that I shall propound to handle is this:

DOCTRINE. There are very many in the world that are almost and, yet, *but almost* Christians. Many are near heaven and, yet, are never the nearer. Many are within a little of salvation and, yet, shall never enjoy the least salvation. They are within sight of heaven and, yet, shall never have a sight of God.

There are two sad expressions in Scripture which I cannot but take notice of in this place. The one is concerning the truly righteous. The other is concerning the seemingly righteous.

It is said of the truly righteous, he shall "scarcely be saved"; and it is said of the seemingly righteous, he shall be "almost saved." "Thou art not far from the kingdom of God."

The righteous shall be saved with a "scarcely"; that is, through much difficulty. He shall go to heaven through many sad fears of hell. The hypocrite shall be saved with an "almost"; that is, he shall go to hell through many fair hopes of heaven.

There are two things which arise from hence of very serious meditation. The one is how often a believer may miscarry - how low he may fall and yet have true grace. The other is how far a hypocrite may go in the way to heaven - how high he may attain and yet have no grace.

The saint may be cast down very near to hell and yet shall never come there, and the hypocrite may be lifted up very near to heaven and yet never come there. The saint may almost perish and yet be saved eternally; the hypocrite may almost be saved and yet perish finally. For the saint at worst is really a believer, and the hypocrite at best is really a sinner.

3 THINGS TO HELP WEAK BELIEVERS

Before I handle the doctrine, I must premise three things which are of great use for the establishing of weak believers that they may not be shaken and discouraged by this doctrine.

1. *There is nothing in the doctrine that should be a matter of stumbling or discouragement to weak Christians.* The gospel does not speak these things to wound believers, but to awaken sinners and formal professors.

As there are none more averse than weak believers to apply the promises and comforts of the gospel to themselves for whom they are properly designed, so there are none more ready than they to apply the threats and severest things of the word to themselves for whom they were never intended. As the disciples, when Christ told them, "One of you shall betray Me"; they that were innocent suspected themselves most and, therefore, cried out, "Master, is it I?" So weak Christians, when they hear sinners reproved or the hypocrite laid open in the ministry of the word, immediately cry out, "Is it I?"

It is the hypocrite's fault to sit under the trials and discoveries of the world and yet not to mind them; and it is the weak Christian's fault to draw sad conclusions of their own state from premises which do not concern them.

There is, indeed, great use of such a doctrine as this to all believers:

To make them look to their standing, upon what foundation they are, and to see that the foundation of their hope be well laid so that they build not upon the sand but upon a rock.

It helps to raise our admiration of the distinguishing love of God in bringing us into the way everlasting when so many perish from the way, and in everpowering our souls into a true conversion when so many take up with a graceless profession.

It incites to that excellent duty of heart-searching so that we approve ourselves to God in sincerity.

It engages the soul in double diligence that it may be found not only believing but persevering in faith to the end.

These duties, and such as these, make this doctrine of use to all believers; but they ought not to make use of it as a stumbling-block in the way of their peace and comfort.

My design in preaching on this subject is not to

make sad the souls of those whom Christ will not have made sad. I would bring water not to quench the flax that is smoking, but to put out that false fire that is of the sinner's own kindling lest, walking all his days by the light thereof, he shall at last lie down in sorrow. My aim is to level the mountain of the sinner's confidence, not to weaken the hand of the believer's faith and dependence; to awaken and bring in secure, formal sinners, not to discourage weak believers.

2. *I would premise this: Though many may go far, very far, in the way to heaven and yet fall short, yet that soul which has the least true grace shall never fall short.* "The righteous shall hold on his way."

Though some may do much in a way of duty, as I shall show hereafter, and yet miscarry, yet that soul which does duty with the least sincerity shall never miscarry, for "He saveth the upright in heart."

The least measure of true grace is as saving as the greatest. It saves as surely, though not as comfortably. The least grace gives a full interest in the blood of Christ whereby we are thoroughly purged, and it gives a full interest in the strength and power of Christ whereby we shall be certainly preserved.

Christ keeps faith in the soul and faith keeps the soul in Christ, and so we are kept by the power of God through faith unto salvation.

3. *I would premise this: They who can hear such truths as this without serious reflection and self-examination, I must suspect the goodness of their condition.*

You will suspect that man to be next door to bankrupt who never casts up his accounts nor looks over his books, and I as verily think that man a hypocrite who never searches nor deals with his own heart.

He who goes on in a road of duties without any un-easiness or doubting of his state, I doubt no man's state more than his.

When we see a man sick and yet not sensible, we conclude the tokens of death are upon him. So, when sinners have no sense of their spiritual condition, it is plain that they are dead in sin. The tokens of eternal death are upon them. These things being premised, which I desire you would carry along in your mind while we travel through this subject, I come to speak to the proposition more distinctly and closely.

DOCTRINE. There are very many in the world who are *almost* **and yet** *but almost* **Christians.** I shall demon-strate the truth of the proposition and then proceed to a more distant prosecution.

I. I shall demonstrate the truth of the proposition, and I shall do it by Scripture-evidence, which speaks plainly and fully to the case.

PROOF 1. The young man in the gospel is an emi-nent proof of this truth. There you read of one who came to Christ to learn of Him the way to heaven. "Good Master, what good thing shall I do, that I may have eternal life?" Our Lord Christ tells him, "If thou wilt enter into life, keep the commandments"; and, when Christ tells him which, he answers, "Lord, all these I have kept from my youth up, what lack I yet?"

Now, see how far this man went.

1. *He obeyed;* he not only heard the commands of God, but he kept them: now, the Scripture says, "Blessed is he that hears the Word of God and keeps it."

2. *He obeyed universally;* not this or that command,

but both this and that. He did not halve it with God, or pick and choose which were easiest to be done and leave the rest. No, but he obeys all. "All these things have I kept."

3. *He obeyed constantly;* not in a fit of zeal only, but in a continual series of duty. His goodness was not, as Ephraim's, "like the morning dew, that passes away." No, "All these things have I kept from my youth up."

4. *He professed his desire to know and do more, to perfect that which was lacking of his obedience;* and, therefore, he goes to Christ to instruct him in his duty. "Master, what lack I yet?" Now, would you not think this a good man? Alas, how few go thus far! And yet, as far as he went, he went not far enough. He was *almost* and yet *but almost* a Christian, for he was an unsound hypocrite. He forsook Christ at last and cleaved to his lust. This, then, is a full proof of the truth of the doctrine.

PROOF 2. A second proof of it is that of the parable of the virgins in St. Matthew. See what a progress they make, how far they go in a profession of Christ.

1. *They are called "virgins."* Now this is a name given in the Scripture, both in the Old Testament and the New, to the saints of Christ. "The virgins love Thee"; so in the Revelation, the "one hundred forty and four thousand" that stood with the Lamb on Mount Zion are called "virgins." They are called virgins because they are not defiled with the corruptions that are in the world through lust. Now, these here seem to be of that sort, for they are called virgins.

2. *They take their lamps;* that is, they make a profession of Christ.

3. *They had some kind of oil in their lamps;* they had some convictions and some faith, though not the faith

of God's elect, to keep their profession alive, to keep the lamp burning.

4. *They went.* Their profession was not an idle profession. They performed duties, frequented ordinances, and did many things commanded. They made a progress – they went.

5. *They went forth.* They went and went out; they left many behind them. This speaks of their separation from the world.

6. *They went with the "wise virgins."* They joined themselves to those who had joined themselves to the Lord, and were companions of them who were companions of Christ.

7. *They went "forth to meet the bridegroom."* This speaks of their owning and seeking after Christ.

8. *When they heard the cry of the bridegroom coming, "they arose and trimmed their lamps."* They professed Christ more highly, hoping now to go in with the bridegroom.

9. *They sought for true grace.* Now, do not we say that the desires of grace are grace? And so they are, if true and timely, if sound and seasonable. Why, here is a desire of grace in these virgins, "Give us of your oil."

It was a desire of true grace, but it was not a true desire of grace. It was not true because not timely; unsound, as being unseasonable; it was too late. Their folly was in not taking oil when they took their lamps. Their time of seeking grace was when they came to Christ. It was too late to seek it when Christ came to them. They should have sought for that when they took up their profession. It was too late to seek it at the coming of the Bridegroom. And, therefore, they were shut out; and though they cried for entrance, "Lord,

Lord, open to us," yet the Lord Christ told them, "I know you not."

You see how far these virgins go in a profession of Jesus Christ, and how long they continue in it even till the bridegroom came; they go to the very door of heaven and there, like the Sodomites, perish with their hands upon the very threshold of glory. They were *almost* Christians, and yet *but almost;* almost saved, and yet they perished.

You who are professors of the gospel of Christ, stand and tremble. If they who have gone beyond us fall short of heaven, what shall become of us who fall short of them? If they who are virgins, who profess Christ, who have some faith in their profession, such as it is, who have some fruit in their faith, who outstrip others who seek Christ, who improve their profession and suit themselves to their profession – nay, who seek grace; if such as these are but *almost* Christians, Lord, what are we?

PROOF 3. If these two witnesses are not sufficient to prove the truth, and confirm the credit of the proposition, take a third; and that shall be from the Old Testament, Isaiah 58:2. See what God said of that people; He gives them a very high character for a choice people, one would think. "They seek Me daily, they delight to know My ways, as a nation that did righteousness, and forsook not the ordinance of their God; they ask of Me the ordinances of justice: they take delight in approaching to God."

See how far these went. If God had not said they were rotten and unsound, we should have taken them for the "he-goats before the flock," and ranked them among the worthies. Pray observe:

1. *They seek God.* Now this is the proper character of a true saint, to seek God. True saints are called "seekers of God." "This is the generation of them that seek him, that seek thy face, O Jacob" (or, O God of Jacob). Lo, here a generation of them that seek God; and are not these the saints of God? Nay, further:

2. *They seek Him daily.* Here is diligence backed with continuance, day by day; that is, every day from day to day. They did not seek Him by fits and starts, nor in a time of trouble and affliction only, as many do. "Lord, in trouble have they visited Thee; they poured out a prayer when Thy chastening was upon them." Many, when God visits them, then they visit Him, but not till then. When God pours out His afflictions, then they pour out their supplications. This is seamen's devotion: when the storms have brought them to their wits' end, then they cry to the Lord in their trouble. Many never cry to God till they are at their wits' end. They never come to God for help as long as they can help themselves. But, now, these here whom God speaks of are more zealous in their devotion. The others make a virtue of necessity, but these seem to make conscience of duty; for, says God, "they seek Me daily." Surely, this is, one would think, a note of sincerity. Job said of the hypocrite, "Will he always call upon God?" Surely not; but now these people call upon God always. They seek Him daily. Certainly these are no hypocrites.

3. *Said God, "They delight to know My ways."* Surely, this frees them from the suspicion of hypocrisy, for they say not unto God, "Depart from us; we desire not the knowledge of Thy ways."

4. *They are as a nation that did righteousness.* Not only as a nation that spake righteousness, knew righteous-

ness, or professed righteousness, but as a nation that did righteousness, that practiced nothing but what was just and right. They appeared, to the judgment of the world, as good as the best.

5. *They forsook not the ordinances of their God.* They seem true to their principles, constant to their profession, better than many among us that cast off duties and forsake the ordinances of God; but these hold out in their profession; they forsook not the ordinances of God.

6. They ask of Me, said God, the ordinances of justice. They will not make their own will the rule of right and wrong, but the law and will of God. *Therefore, in all their dealings with men, they desire to be guided and counselled by God.* They ask of Me the ordinances of justice.

7. *They take delight in approaching God.* Surely this cannot be the guise of a hypocrite. "Will he delight himself in the Almighty?" said Job. No, he will not. Though God is the chief delight of man (having every thing in Him to render Him lovely, as was said of Titus Vespasian), yet the hypocrites will not delight in God. Till the affections are made spiritual, there is no affection to things that are spiritual. God is a spiritual good and, therefore, hypocrites cannot delight in God. But these are a people that delight in approaching to God.

8. *They were a people that were much in fasting.* "Wherefore had we fasted," say they, "and Thou seest not?" Now, this is a duty that does not suppose and require truth of grace only in the heart, but strength of grace.

"No man," said our Lord Christ, "puts new wine into old bottles, lest the bottles break and the wine run out." New wine is strong and old bottles weak, and the strong wine breaks the weak vessels. This is a reason Christ gives why His disciples, who were newly converted and but weak as yet, were not exercised with this austere discipline. But this people here mentioned were a people that fasted often, afflicted their souls much, and wore themselves out by frequent practices of humiliation. Surely, therefore, this was "new wine in new bottles." This must be a people strong in grace. There seems to be grace not only in truth, but also in growth. And yet, for all this, they were no better than a generation of hypocrites. They made a goodly progress and went far, but yet they went not far enough. They were cast off by God after all.

I hope by this time the truth of the point is sufficiently avouched and confirmed, that a man may be, yea, very many are, *almost*, and yet not more than *but almost* Christians.

II. Now, for the more distinct prosecution of the point:

1. I shall show you, step by step, how far he may go, to what attainments he may reach, how specious and singular a progress he may make in religion, and yet be but *almost* a Christian when all is done.

2. I will show whence it is that many men go so far as that they are *almost* Christians.

3. Why they are but *almost* Christians when they have gone thus far.

4. What the reason is why men who go thus far as to be *almost* Christians yet go no further than to be *almost* Christians.

Question 1

How far may a man go in the way to heaven and yet be but almost a Christian?

This I will show you in twenty steps.

SECTION 1. A man may have much knowledge and much light; he may know much of God and His will, much of Christ and His ways, and yet be but almost a Christian. For, though there can be no grace without knowledge, yet there may be much knowledge where there is no grace. Illumination often goes before when conversion never follows after. The subject of knowledge is the understanding; the subject of holiness is the will. Now, a man may have his understanding enlightened and yet his will not at all sanctified. He may have an understanding to know God and yet lack a will to obey God. The apostle tells us of some that "when they knew God, they glorified him not as God."

To make a man altogether a Christian, there must be light in the head and heat in the heart, knowledge in the understanding and zeal in the affections. Some have zeal and no knowledge - that is blind devotion. Some have knowledge and no zeal - that is fruitless speculation. But where knowledge is joined with zeal, that makes a true Christian.

OBJECTION. But is it not said, "This is life eternal, to know Thee, the only true God, and Jesus Christ whom Thou hast sent?"

ANSWER. It is not every knowledge of God and

16

Christ that interests the soul in life eternal. For why, then, do the devils perish? They have more knowledge of God than all the men in the world; for though, by their fall, they lost their holiness, yet they lost not their knowledge. They are called *daimones* from their knowledge, and yet they are *diaboloi* from their malice, devils still.

Knowledge may fill the head, but it will never better the heart if there is not something else. The Pharisees had much knowledge. "Behold, thou art called a Jew, and restest in the law, and makes thy boast of God, and knowest his will," etc., and yet they were a generation of hypocrites. Alas, how many have gone loaded with knowledge to hell!

Though it is true that it is life eternal to know God and Jesus Christ, yet it is as true that many know God and Jesus Christ that shall never see life eternal. There is, you must know, a twofold knowledge: the one is common, but not saving; the other is not common, but saving. Common knowledge is that which floats in the head but does not influence the heart. This knowledge reprobates may have; Balaam saw Christ from the top of the rocks, and from the hills.

Naturalists say that there is a pearl in the toad's head and yet her belly is full of poison. The French have a berry which they call *uve de spine*, the grape of a thorn. The common knowledge of Christ is the pearl in the toad's head, the grape that grows upon thorns; it may be found in men unsanctified.

And then there is a saving knowledge of God and Christ which includes the assent of the mind and the consent of the will. This is a knowledge that implies faith. "By His knowledge shall My righteous Servant justify many." And this is that knowledge which leads to life eternal. Now, whatever that measure of knowledge is which a man may have of God and of Jesus Christ, yet, if it is not this saving knowledge, knowledge joined with affection and application, he is but almost a Christian.

He only knows God aright who knows how to obey Him, and obeys according to his knowledge of Him. "A good understanding have all they that do His commandments." All knowledge without this makes a man but like Nebuchadnezzar's image, with "a head of gold, and feet of clay."

Some know merely to know. Some know to be known. Some know to practice what they know.

Now to know but to know is curiosity To know to be known is vain glory. But to know to practice what we know is gospel-duty. This makes a man a complete Christian. The other, without this, makes a man almost and yet but almost a Christian.

SECTION II. A man may have great and eminent gifts, yea, spiritual gifts, and yet be but almost a Christian.

The gift of prayer is a spiritual gift. Now this a man may have and yet be but almost a Christian, for the gift of prayer is one thing, the grace of prayer is another. The gift of preaching and prophesying is a spiritual gift. Now, this a man may have and yet be but almost a Christian. Judas was a great preacher; so were they that came to Christ and said, "Lord, Lord, we have prophesied in Thy name, and in Thy name have cast out devils."

You must know that it is not gifts, but grace, which

makes a Christian. For:

1. *Gifts are from a common work of the Spirit.* Now a man may partake of all the common gifts of the Spirit and yet be a reprobate; for, therefore, they are called common because they are indifferently dispensed by the Spirit to good and bad, to those that are believers and to those that are not.

They that have grace have gifts; and they that have no grace may have the same gifts for the Spirit works in both. Nay, in this sense, he that has no grace is under a greater work of the Spirit (*quoad hoc*) as to this thing than he that has most grace. A graceless professor may have greater gifts than the most holy believer; he may out-pray, out-preach, and out-do them, but they, in sincerity and integrity, out-go him.

2. *Gifts are for the use and good of others.* They are given *in ordinem alium,* as the schoolmen speak, for the profiting and edifying of others. So says the apostle, "they are given to profit withal." Now a man may edify another by his gifts and yet be unedified himself. He may be profitable to another and yet unprofitable to himself.

The raven was an unclean bird. God made use of her to feed Elijah. Though she was not good meat, yet it was good meat she brought. A lame man may, with his crutch, point you to the right way and yet not be able to walk in it himself. A crooked tailor may make a suit to fit a straight body, though it does not fit him that made it because of his crookedness. The church (Christ's garden enclosed) may be watered through a wooden gutter, the sun may give light through a dusky window, and the field may be well sowed with a dirty hand.

The efficacy of the Word does not depend upon the authority of him that speaks it, but upon the authority of God that blesses it. So that another may be converted by my preaching and yet I may be cast away, notwithstanding. Balaam makes a clear and rare prophecy of Christ and yet he has no benefit by Christ: "there shall come a star out of Jacob, and a sceptre shall rise out of Israel;" but yet Balaam shall have no benefit by it. "I shall see Him, but not now; I shall behold Him, but not nigh."

God may use a man's gifts to bring another to Christ when he himself, whose gifts God uses, may be a stranger unto Christ. One man may confirm another in the faith and yet himself may be a stranger to the faith. Pendleton strengthened and confirmed Sanders, in Queen Mary's days, to stand in the truth he had preached and to seal it with his blood, and yet, afterwards, played the apostate himself.

Scultetus tells us of one Johannes Speiserus, a famous preacher of Augsburgh in Germany in the year 1523, who preached the gospel so powerfully that divers common harlots were converted and became good Christians; and yet himself afterwards turned papist and came to a miserable end. Thus the candle may burn bright to light others in their world and yet, afterwards, go out in a stink.

3. *It is beyond the power of the greatest gifts to change the heart.* A man may preach like an apostle, pray like an angel, and yet may have the heart of a devil. It is grace only that can change the heart. The greatest gifts cannot change it, but the least grace can. Gifts may make a man a scholar, but grace makes a man a believer. Now, if gifts cannot change the heart, then a man may have

the greatest gifts and yet be but almost a Christian.

4. *Many have gone laden with gifts to hell.* No doubt Judas had great gifts, for he was a preacher of the gospel; and our Lord Jesus Christ would not set him to work and not fit him for the work, yet "Judas is gone to his own place." The Scribes and Pharisees were men of great gifts and yet, "Where is the wise? Where is the scribe?"

"The preaching of the cross is to them that perish foolishness." They that perish, who are they? Who? The wise and the learned, both among the Jews and Greeks. These are called "they that perish." A great bishop said, when he saw a poor shepherd weeping over a toad, "The poor illiterate world attain to heaven, while we, with all our learning, fall into hell."

There are three things must be done for us if ever we would avoid perishing:

We must be thoroughly convinced of sin.

We must be really united to Christ.

We must be instated in the covenant of grace.

Now, the greatest gifts cannot stead us in any of these.

They cannot work thorough convictions.

They cannot effect our union.

They cannot bring us into covenant-relation. And, consequently, they cannot preserve us from eternally perishing; and, if so, then many may have the greatest gifts and yet be but almost a Christian.

5. *Gifts may decay and perish.* They do not lie beyond the reach of corruption. Indeed, grace shall never perish, but gifts will. Grace is incorruptible though gifts are not. Grace "is a spring whose waters fail not," but the streams of gifts may be dried up. If grace is cor-

ruptible in its own nature, as being but a creature, yet it is incorruptible in regard of its Conserver, as being the new creature. He that created it in us will conserve it in us; he that began it will also finish it.

Gifts have their root in nature, but grace has its roots in Christ; and, therefore, though gifts may die and whither, yet grace shall abide forever. Now, if gifts are perishing, then, though he that has the least grace is a Christian, he that has the greatest gifts may be but almost a Christian.

OBJECTION. But does not the apostle bid us to "covet earnestly the best gifts?" Why must we covet them, and covet them earnestly, if they do not avail to salvation?

ANSWER. Gifts are good, though they are not the best good. They are excellent, but there is something more excellent. So it follows in the same verse, "Yet I show unto you a more excellent way," and that is the way of grace. One dram of grace is more worth than a talent of gifts. Gifts may make us rich towards men, but it is grace that makes us rich towards God. Our gifts profit others, but grace profits ourselves. That whereby I profit another is good, but that by which I am profited myself is better.

Now, because gifts are good, therefore, we ought to covet them. But, because they are not the best good, therefore, we ought not to rest in them. We must covet gifts for the good of others that they may be edified, and we must covet grace for the good of our own souls that they may be saved; for whoever may be bettered by our gifts, yet we shall miscarry without grace.

SECTION III. **A man may have a high profession of religion, be much in external duties of godliness, and yet be but almost a Christian.**

Mark what our Lord tells them, "Not every one who saith unto me, Lord, Lord, shall enter into the kingdom of heaven"; that is, not every one who makes a profession of Christ shall, therefore, be owned for a true disciple of Christ. All are not Israel who are of Israel; nor all Christians who make a profession of religion.

What a godly profession Judas had! He followed Christ, left all for Christ, preached the gospel of Christ, cast out devils in the name of Christ, and ate and drank at the table of Christ, yet Judas was only a hypocrite.

Most professors are like lilies: fair in show, but foul in scent; or like pepper: hot in the mouth, but cold in the stomach. The finest lace may be upon the coarsest cloth.

It is a great deceit to measure the substance of our religion by the bulk of our profession, and to judge of the strength of our graces by the length of our duties. The Scriptures speak of some who, having a form of godliness, yet deny the power thereof. They deny the power; that is, they do not live in the practice of those graces to which they pretend in their duties. He who pretends to godliness by a specious profession, and yet does not practice godliness by a holy conversation, has a form, but denies the power. Grotius compares such to the ostrich which has great wings but yet does not fly. Many have the wings of a fair profession but yet do not use them to mount upward in spiritual affections and a heavenly conversation.

FOUR EVIDENCES OF THIS TRUTH

But to clear the truth of this, that a man may make a high profession of religion and yet be but almost a Christian, take a fourfold evidence:

1. *If a man may profess religion and yet never have his heart changed nor his state bettered, then he may be a great professor and yet be but almost a Christian.* But a man may profess religion and yet never have his heart changed nor his state renewed. He may be a constant hearer of the Word and yet be a sinner still. He may come often to the Lord's table and yet go away a sinner as he came. We must not think that duties can confer grace.

Many a soul has been converted by Christ in an ordinance, but never was any soul converted by an ordinance without Christ. And does Christ convert all that sit under the ordinances? Surely not; for to some, *the Word is a savour of death unto death.* And, if so, then it is plain that a man may profess religion and yet be but almost a Christian.

2. *A man may profess religion and live in a form of godliness in hypocrisy.* "Hear ye this, O house of Jacob, which are called by the name of Israel, and are come forth out of the waters of Judah; which swear by the name of the Lord, and make mention of the God of Israel, but not in truth, nor in righteousness." What do you think of these? "They make mention of the name of the Lord" – there is their profession; "but not in truth, nor in righteousness" – there is their dissimulation. And, indeed, there could be no hypocrisy in a religious sense were it not for a profession of religion; for he that is wicked, carnal, and vile inwardly, and appears to be so outwardly, is no hypocrite, but is what he

appears and appears what he is. But he that is one thing really, and another thing seemingly, is carnal and unholy, and yet seems to be good and holy – he is a hypocrite.

Thus the casuists define hypocrisy to be a counterfeiting of holiness; and this fits exactly with the Greek word, which is to counterfeit. And, to this purpose, the Hebrews have two words for hypocrites; *panim,* which signifies "faces"; and *chanepim,* which signifies "counterfeits"; from *chanaph,* to dissemble. So he is a hypocrite who dissembles religion and wears the face of holiness and yet is without the grace of holiness. He appears to be in semblance what he is not in substance. He wears a form of godliness without, only as a cover of a profane heart within. He has a profession that he may not be thought wicked, but it is but a profession and, therefore, he is wicked. He is the religious hypocrite - religious, because he merely pretends to it. He is like many men in a consumption who have fresh looks and yet rotten lungs, or like an apple that has a fair skin but a rotten core. Many appear righteous who are only righteous in appearance. And, if so, then a man may profess religion and yet be but almost a Christian.

3. *Custom and fashion may make a man a professor; as you have many that wear this or that garb, not because it keeps them warmer or has an excellency in it more than another, but merely for fashion.*

Many must have powdered hair, spotted faces, feathers in their caps, etc., for no other end but because they would be fools in fashion. So, many profess Christianity not because the means of grace warm the heart, or that they see any excellencies in the ways of

God above the world, but merely to follow the fashion!
I wish I might not say it has been true of our days because religion has been uppermost; therefore, many
have professed. It has been the gaining trade and,
then, most will be of that trade.

Religion in credit makes many professors but few
proselytes; but when religion suffers, then its confessors are no more than its converts, for custom makes
the former, but conscience the latter. He that is a professor of religion merely for custom's sake, when it
prospers, will never be a martyr for Christ's sake when
religion suffers. He that owns the truth to live upon it
will disown it when it comes to live upon him.

They say that, when a house is decaying or falling,
all the rats and mice will forsake it. While the house is
firm and they may shelter in the roof, they will stay, but
no longer, lest, in the decay, the fall should be upon
them and they that lived at top should die at bottom.
My brethren, may I not say we have many who are the
vermin, the rats and mice of religion, who would live
under the roof of it while they might have shelter in it;
but, when it suffers, they forsake it lest it should fall
and the fall should be upon them? I am persuaded this
is not the least reason why God has brought the wheel
upon the profession of religion, namely, to rid it of the
vermin. He shakes the foundations of the house that
these rats and mice may quit the roof; not to overturn
it, but to rid them of it, as the husbandman fans the
wheat that he may get rid of the chaff. The halcyon
days of the gospel provoke hypocrisy, but the sufferings
for religion prove sincerity.

Now, then, if custom and fashion make many men
professors, then a man may profess religion and yet be

but almost a Christian.

4. *If many may perish under a profession of godliness, then a man may profess religion and yet be but almost a Christian.*

Now, the Scripture is clear that a man may perish under the highest profession of religion. Christ cursed the fig-tree that had leaves and no fruit. It is said, that "the children of the kingdom shall be cast out into outer darkness." Who were these but they that were then the only people of God in the world by profession; that had made a "covenant with Him by sacrifice!" and yet these were cast out.

In St. Matthew, you read of some who came and made boast of their profession to Christ, hoping that might save them. "Lord," say they, "have we not prophesied in Thy name, cast out devils in Thy name, done many wonderful works in Thy name?" Now what does our Lord Christ say to this? "Then I will profess unto them, I never knew you; depart from Me."

Mark, here are they who prophesy in His name and yet perish in His wrath; in His name cast out devils and then are cast out themselves; in His name do many wonderful works and yet perish as wicked workers. The profession of religion will no more keep a man from perishing than calling a ship the Safeguard or the Good-speed will keep her from sinking. As many go to heaven with the fear of hell in their hearts, so many go to hell with the name of Christ in their mouths. Now, then, if many may perish under a profession of godliness, then a man may be a high professor of religion and yet be but almost a Christian.

OBJECTION. But is it not said by the Lord Christ Himself, "He that confesses Me before men, him will I confess before My Father in heaven?" Now, for Christ to say that He will confess us before the Father is equivalent to a promise of eternal life for, if Christ confesses us, God the Father will never disown us.

True, they who confess Christ shall be confessed by Him, and it is as true that this confession is equivalent to a promise of salvation. But now you must know that professing Christ is not confessing Him, for to profess Christ is one thing; to confess Christ is another. Confession is a living testimony for Christ in a time when religion suffers. Profession may be only a lifeless formality in a time when religion prospers. To confess Christ is to choose His ways and own them. To profess Christ is to plead for His ways and yet live beside them. Profession may be from a feigned love to the ways of Christ, but confession is from a rooted love to the person of Christ. To profess Christ is to own Him when none deny Him; to confess Christ is to plead for Him and suffer for Him when others oppose Him. Hypocrites may be professors, but the martyrs are the true confessors. Profession is swimming down the stream. Confession is a swimming against the stream. Now, many may swim with the stream like the dead fish that cannot swim against the stream with the living fish. Many may profess Christ that cannot confess Christ; and so these, notwithstanding their profession, yet are but almost Christians.

SECTION IV. **To come yet nearer, a man may go far in opposing his sin and yet be but almost a Christian.**

How far a man may go in this work, I shall show you in seven gradual instances:

First, a man may be convinced of sin and yet be but almost a Christian, for:

1. *Conviction may be rational as well as spiritual.* It may be from a natural conscience enlightened by the Word without the effectual work of the Spirit applying sin to the heart.

2. *Convictions may be worn out.* They, many times, go off and do not end in sound conversion. The church says, "We have been with child; we have been in pain; we have brought forth wind." This is the complaint of the Church in reference to the unprofitableness of their afflictions, and it may be the complaint of most in reference to the unprofitableness of their convictions.

3. *Many take conviction of sin to be conversion from sin and so sit down and rest in their convictions.* It is a sad complaint God makes of Ephraim, "Ephraim is an unwise son; for he should not stay long in the place of the breaking forth of children." Now, then, if convictions may be only from natural conscience, if they may be worn out or mistaken and rested in for conversion, then a man may have convictions and be but almost a Christian.

Second, a man may mourn for sin and yet be but almost a Christian. So did Saul; so did Esau for the loss of his birthright, which was his sin and, therefore, he is called by the Spirit of God, "profane Esau"; yet, "he sought it again carefully with tears."

OBJECTION. But does not Christ pronounce them blessed that mourn? "Blessed are they that mourn". Surely, then, if a man mourns for sin, he is in a good condition. You see, said Nazianzen, that salvation is joined with sorrow.

SOLUTION. I answer, it is true that they who mourn for sin in the sense Christ there speaks of are blessed, but all mourning for sin does not, therefore, render us blessed.

1. *True mourning for sin must flow from spiritual convictions of the evil, vileness, and damnable nature of sin.* Now, all who mourn for sin do not do it from a thorough work of spiritual conviction upon the soul. They do not have a right sense of the evil and vileness of sin.

2. *True mourning for sin is more for the evil that is in sin than the evil that comes by sin; more because it dishonors God, wounds Christ, grieves the Spirit, and makes the soul unlike God than because it damns the soul.* Now, there are many who mourn for sin, not so much for the evil that is in it as for the evil that it brings with it. There is mourning for sin in hell. You read of "weeping and wailing" there. The damned are weeping and mourning to eternity. There is all sorrow and no comfort. As in heaven there is peace without trouble and joy without mourning, so in hell there is trouble without peace, mourning without joy, weeping and wailing incessantly; but it is for the evil they feel by sin and not for the evil that is in sin. So a man may mourn for sin and yet be but almost a Christian. It may grieve him to think of perishing for sin when it does not grieve him that he is defiled and polluted by sin.

Third, a man may make large confession of sin to God and to others and yet be but almost a Christian. How ingenuously does Saul confess his sin to David! "I have sinned," said he, "thou art more righteous than I. Behold, I have played the fool, and have erred exceedingly." So Judas makes a full confession, "I have sinned in betraying innocent blood." Yet Saul and Judas were both rejected of God. So a man may confess sin and yet be but almost a Christian.

OBJECTION. But is not confession of sin a character of a child of God? Does not the apostle say, "If we confess our sins, God is just and faithful to forgive them?" No man was ever kept out of heaven for his confessed badness, though many are kept out of heaven for their supposed goodness. Judah, in Hebrew, signifies "confession." Now, Judah got the kingdom from Reuben; confession of sin is the way to the kingdom of heaven.

ANSWER. There are some who confess sin and are saved; there are others who confess sin and perish.

Many confess sin merely out of custom and not out of conscience. You may have many that will never pray, but they will make a long confession of sin and yet never feel the weight or burden of it upon their consciences.

Many will confess lesser sins and yet conceal greater; like the patient in Plutarch who complained to his physician of his finger when his liver was rotten.

Many will confess sin in general, or confess themselves sinners, and yet see little, and say less, of their particular sins. An implicit confession, as one said, is almost as bad as an implicit faith.

Where confession is right, it will be distinct, especially of those sins that were our chief sins. So David confesses his blood-guiltiness and adultery; so Paul his blasphemy, persecution, and injury against the saints. It is bad to hear men confess they are great sinners who yet cannot confess their sins. Though the least sin is too bad to be committed, yet there is no sin too bad to be confessed.

Many will confess sin, but it is only under extremity; that is not free and voluntary. Pharaoh confessed his sin, but it was when judgment compelled him. "I have sinned against the Lord," said he, but it was when he had had eight plagues upon him.

Many do, by their sins, as mariners do by their goods - cast them out in a storm, wishing for them again in a calm. Confession should come like water out of a spring which runs freely, not like water out of a still which is forced by fire.

Many confess their sins, but with no intent to forsake sin. They confess the sins they have committed, but do not leave the sins they have confessed.

Many men use their confession as Lewis the XI of France did his crucifix. He would swear an oath and then kiss it, and swear again and then kiss it again. So, many sin and then confess they do not do well, but yet never strive to do better.

Mr. Torshel tells a story of a minister he knew that would often be drunk and, when he came into the pulpit, would confess it very lamentingly. Yet no sooner was he out of the pulpit but he would be drunk again, and this would he do as constantly as men follow their trades.

Now, then, if a man may confess sin merely out of

custom; if he may confess lesser sins and yet conceal greater; if he may confess sin only in the general, or only under extremity; or if he may confess sin without any intent to forsake sin; then, surely, a man may confess sin and yet be but almost a Christian.

Fourth, a man may forsake sin and yet be but almost a Christian. He may leave his lust and his wicked ways which he sometimes lived in and, in the judgment of the world, become a new man and yet not be a new creature. Simon Magus, when he heard Philip preaching concerning the kingdom of God, left his sorcery and witchcraft and believed.

OBJECTION. But you will say, "This seems contrary to Scripture, for that says, 'He that confesseth and forsaketh sin shall have mercy.' But I confess sin; yea, not only so, but also I forsake sin. Surely, therefore, this mercy is my portion. It belongs to me."

ANSWER. It is true that where a soul forsakes sin from a right principle, after a right manner, to a right end; where he forsakes sin as sin, as being contrary to God, and the purity of his nature, this declares that soul to be right with God; and the promise shall be made good to it: "He shall find mercy."

But, now, mind that there is a forsaking sin that is not right, but unsound.

1. *Open sins may be deserted and yet secret sins may be retained.* Now, this is not a right forsaking. Such a soul shall never find mercy. A man may be cured of a wound in the flesh and yet may die of an abcess in his bowels.

2. *A man may forsake sin but not as sin, for he that for-*

sakes sin as sin forsakes all sin. It is impossible for a man to forsake sin as sin unless he forsakes all that he knows to be sin.

3. *A man may let one sin go to hold another the faster.* A man who goes to sea would willingly save all his goods; but, if the storm arises so that he cannot, then he throws some overboard to lighten the vessel and save the rest. So did they, Acts 27:38. So the sinner chooses to keep all his sins; but, if a storm arises in his conscience, why, then, he will heave one lust overboard to save the life of another.

4. *A man may let all sin go and yet be a sinner still; for there is the root of all sin in the heart though the fruit is not seen in the life.* The tree lives though the boughs are lopped off. As a man is a sinner before ever he acts sin, so (till grace renews him) he is a sinner though he leaves sin; for there is original sin in him enough to damn and destroy him.

5. *Sin may be left and yet be loved.* A man may forsake the life of sin and yet retain the love of sin. Now, though leaving sin makes him almost a Christian, yet loving sin shows he is but almost a Christian. It is less evil to do sin and not love it than to love sin and not do it, for to do sin may argue only weakness of grace, but to love sin argues strength of lust. "What I hate, that I do." Sin is bad in any part of man, but sin in the affection is worse than sin in the conversation; for sin in the conversation may be only from infirmity, but sin in the affection is the fruit of choice and unregeneracy.

6. *All sin may be chained and yet the heart not changed;* and so the nature of the sinner is the same as ever. A dog chained up is a dog still, as much as if he was let loose to devour.

There may be a cessation of arms between enemies and yet the quarrel may remain on foot still. There may be a making truce where there is no making peace.

A sinner may lay the weapons of sin out of his hand and yet the enmity against God still remain in his heart. There may be a truce. He may not sin against Him, but there can be no peace till he is united to Him.

Restraining grace holds in the sinner, but it is renewing grace that changes his nature. Now, many are held in by grace from being open sinners who are not renewed by grace and made true believers.

Now, then, if a man may forsake open sins and retain secret sins; if he may forsake sin but not as sin; if he may let one sin go to hold another the faster; if a man may let all sin go and yet be a sinner still; if sin may be left and yet be loved; finally, if all sin may be chained and yet the heart not changed, then a man may forsake sin and yet be but almost a Christian

SECTION V. A man may hate sin, and yet be but almost a Christian. Absalom hated Amnon's uncleanness with his sister Tamar. Yea, his hatred was so great that he slew him for it, and yet Absalom was but a wicked man.

OBJECTION. But the Scripture makes it a sign of a gracious heart to hate sin. Yea, though a man through infirmities falls into sin, yet, if he hates it, this is a proof of grace. Paul proves the sincerity of his heart and the truth of his grace by this hatred of sin, though he committed it. "What I hate, that I do." Nay, what is grace but a conformity of the soul to God; to love as God loves, to hate as God hates? Now, God hates sin. It is one part of His holiness to hate all sin. And if I hate sin, then am I conformed to God; and, if I am conformed to God, then am I altogether a Christian.

ANSWER. It is true that there is a hatred of sin which is a sign of grace, which flows from a principle of grace, and is grace. For instance, to hate sin as it is an offense to God, a wrong to His majesty; to hate sin as it is a breach of the command, and so a wicked controlling of God's will which is the only rule of goodness; to hate sin as being a disingenuous transgression of that law of love established in the blood and death of Christ, and so, in a degree, a crucifying of Christ afresh; to hate sin as being a grieving and quenching the Spirit of God as all sin in its nature is. Thus, to hate sin is grace, and thus every true Christian hates sin.

But, though every man who has grace hates sin, yet every man who hates sin does not have grace; for a man may hate sin from other principles - not as it is a wrong to God, or wounding Christ, or grieving the Spirit, for then he would hate all sin. There is no sin that does not have this in its nature, but:

1. *A man may hate sin for the shame that attends it more than for the evil that is in it.* There are some sinners "who declare their sin as Sodom and hide it not." They are set down in the seat of the scornful; "they glory in their shame." But now, there are others who are ashamed of sin and, therefore, hate it, not for the sin's sake, but for the shame's sake. This made Absalom hate Amnon's uncleanness, because it brought shame upon him and his sister.

2. *A man may hate sin more in others than in himself.* So

does the drunkard - he hates drunkenness in another and yet practices it himself. The liar hates falsehood in another but likes it himself. Now, he who hates sin from a principle of grace hates sin most in himself. He hates sin in others, but he loathes most the sins of his own heart.

3. *A man may hate one sin as being contrary to another.* There is a great contrariety between sin and sin, between lust and lust. It is the excellency of the life of grace that it is a uniform life. There is no one grace contrary to another. The graces of God's Spirit are different but not differing. Faith, love, and holiness are all one. They consist together at the same time in the same subject. Nay, they cannot be parted. There can be no faith without love, no love without holiness, and so, on the other hand, no holiness without love, no love without faith. This makes the life of grace an easy and excellent life; but, now, the life of sin is a distracting, contradictory life wherein a man is a servant to contrary lusts. The lust of pride and prodigality is contrary to the lust of covetousness, etc. Now, where one lust gets to be the master-lust of the soul, then that works a hatred of its contrary. Where covetousness gets the heart, there the heart hates pride; and where pride gets uppermost in the heart, there the heart hates covetousness. Thus, a man may hate sin not from a principle of grace but from the contrariety of lust. He does not hate any sin as it is sin, but he hates it as being contrary to his beloved sin.

Now, then, if a man may hate sin for the shame that attends it, if he may hate sin more in others than in himself, if he may hate one sin as being contrary to another, then he may hate sin and yet be but almost a

Christian.

SECTION VI. A man may make great vows and promises; he may have strong purposes and resolutions against sin, and yet be but almost a Christian.

Thus did Saul. He promised and resolved against his sin, "Return, my son David," said he, "for I will no more do thee harm." What promises and resolves Pharaoh made against that sin of detaining God's people! Said he, "I will let the people go that they may do sacrifice to the Lord." And again, "I will let you go and ye shall stay no longer." And yet Saul and Pharaoh both perished in their sins. The greatest purposes and promises against sin will not make a man a Christian, for:

1. *Purposes and promises against sin never hurt sin.* We say, "threatened folks live long"; and, truly, so do threatened sins. It is not new purposes, but a new nature, that must help us against sin. Purposes may bring us to the place of giving birth, but, without a new nature, there is no strength to bring forth. The new nature is the best soil for holy purposes to grow in; otherwise, they wither and die like plants in an improper soil.

2. *Troubles and afflictions may provoke us to large purposes and promises against sin for the future.* What is more common than to vow and not to pay? To make vows in the day of trouble which we make no conscience to pay in the day of grace? Many covenant against sin when trouble is upon them and then sin against their covenant when it is removed from them. It was a brave rule that Pliny, in one of his epistles, gave his friend to live by, "We should continue to be such when we are

well as we promise to be when we are sick." Many are
our sickbed promises, but we are no sooner well than
we grow sick of our promises.

3. *Purposes and resolves against sin for the future may be
only a temptation to put off repentance for the present.* Satan
may put a man on to good purposes to keep him from
present attempts. He knows whatever we purpose, yet
the strength of performance is not in ourselves. He
knows that purposes for the future are putting God off
for the present. They are a secret "will-not" to a present
opportunity. That is a notable passage, "Follow me,"
said Christ to the two men. Now, see what answers they
gave to Christ. "Suffer me first to go and bury my father," says one. This man purposes to follow Christ,
only he would stay to bury his father. Says the other,
"Lord, I will follow Thee, but let me first go and bid
them farewell which are at my house." I will follow
Thee, but only I would first go and take my leave of my
friends, or set my house in order: and yet we do not
find that they ever followed Christ, notwithstanding
their fair purposes.

4. *Nature unsanctified may be so far wrought on as to
make great promises and purposes against sin.*

First, a natural man may have great convictions of
sin from the workings of an enlightened conscience.

Second, he may approve of the law of God.

Third, he may have a desire to be saved.

Now these three together, the workings of conscience, the sight of the goodness of the law, and a desire to be saved, may bring forth in a man great purposes against sin and yet he may have no heart to perform his own purposes, This was much like the case of
those who said to Moses, "Go thou near, and hear all

that the Lord our God shall say; and tell thou it to us, and we will hear it, and do it." This is a fair promise and so God takes it. "I have heard the words of this people; they have well said all they have spoken." So said and so done would have been well, but it was better said than done; for, though they had a tongue to promise, yet had they no heart to perform. This God saw and, therefore, said He, "O that there were such an heart in them that they would fear Me, and keep My commandments always, that it might be well with them!" They promised to fear God and keep His commandments, but they lacked a new heart to perform what an unsanctified heart had promised. It fares with men in this case as it did with that son in the gospel who said he would go into the vineyard but went not.

Now, then, if purposes and promises against sin never hurt sin; if present afflictions may draw out large promises; if they may be the fruit of a temptation, or if from nature unsanctified; surely, then, a man may promise and purpose much against sin and yet be but almost a Christian.

SECTION VII. A man may maintain a strife and combat against sin in himself, and yet be but almost a Christian.

So did Balaam: when he went to curse the people of God, he had a great strife within himself. "How shall I curse, said he, whom God hath not cursed? or how shall I defy whom the Lord hath not defied?" And did not Pilate strive against his sin when he said to the Jews, "Shall I crucify your king? What evil hath He done? I am innocent of the blood of this just man."

OBJECTION. But you will say, "Is not this an argument of grace, when there is a striving in the soul against sin? For what should oppose sin in the heart but grace? The apostle makes the lusting of the flesh against the Spirit and the Spirit against the flesh to be an argument of grace in the heart. Now I find this strife in my heart; though the remainders of corruption sometimes break out into actual sins, yet I find a striving in my soul against sin."

ANSWER. It is true that there is a striving against sin which is only from grace, and is proper to believers; and there is a striving against sin which is not from grace and, therefore, may be in them that are not believers. There is a strife against sin in one and the same faculty; the will against the will, the affection against the affection, and this is that which the apostle calls "the lusting of the flesh against the Spirit," that is, the striving of the unregenerate part against the regenerate. And this is ever in the same faculty, and is proper to believers only.

An unbeliever never finds this strife in himself. This strife cannot be in him. It is impossible as such; that is, while he is on this side of a state of grace. But, then, there is a striving against sin in divers faculties, and this is the strife that is in them who are not believers. There, the strife is between the will and the conscience; conscience enlightened and terrified with the fear of hell and damnation, that is against sin; the will and affection, not being renewed, are for sin. And this causes great tugging and combats, many times, in the sinner's heart. Thus it was with the Scribes and Pharisees. Conscience convinced them of the divinity of Christ and the truth of His being the Son of God, and yet a perverse will and carnal affections cry out, "Crucify Him! Crucify Him!" Conscience pleaded for Him. He had a witness in their bosoms, and yet their wills were bent against Him and, therefore, they are said to have "resisted the Spirit", namely, the workings and convictions of the Spirit in their consciences.

This is the case of many sinners. When the will and affections are for sin and plead for it, conscience is against it and, many times, frightens the soul from the doing of it. Hence, men take that which opposes sin in them to be grace when it is only the work of a natural conscience. They conclude the strife is between grace and sin, the regenerate and unregenerate part, when, alas, it is no other than the contention of a natural conscience against a corrupt will and corrupt affections! And, if so, then a man may have great strifes and combats against sin in him and yet be but almost a Christian.

A man may desire grace and yet be but almost a Christian. So did the five foolish virgins, "Give us of your oil." What was that but true grace? It was that oil that lit the wise virgins into the bridegroom's chamber. They not only desired to enter in, but they desired oil to light them in. Wicked men may desire heaven and Christ to save them. There is none so wicked upon earth who does not desire to be happy in heaven. But, now, here are they who desire grace as well as glory, and yet these are but almost Christians.

OBJECTION. But is it not commonly taught that desires of grace are grace? Nay, does not our Lord Christ make it so? "Blessed are they that hunger and thirst after righteousness; for they shall be filled."

ANSWER. It is true that there are some desires of grace which are grace, as:

1. *When a man desires grace from a right sense of his natural state*; when he sees the vileness of sin and the woeful, defiled, and loathsome condition he is in by reason of sin and, therefore, desires the grace of Christ to renew and change him, this is grace. This some make to be the lowest degree of saving faith.

2. *When a man joins proportionable endeavors to his desires not only wishes for grace, but works for grace, such desires are grace.*

3. *When a man's desires are constant and incessant, that cease not but in the attainment of their object, such desires are true grace.* They are a part of the special work of the Spirit. They really partake of the nature of grace. Now it is a known maxim, "that which partakes of the nature of the whole is a part of the whole." The fillings of gold are gold. The sea is not more really water than the least drop. The flame is not more really fire than the least spark.

But, though all true desires of grace are grace, yet all desire of grace are not true, for:

1) A man may desire grace not for itself, but for something else; not for grace's sake, but for heaven's sake. He does not desire grace that his nature may be changed, his heart renewed, the image of God stamped upon him, and his lusts subdued in him. These are blessed desires found only in true believers. The true Christian only can desire grace for grace's sake, but the almost Christian may desire grace for heaven's sake.

2) A man may desire grace without proportionable endeavors after grace. Many are good at wish-

ing, but bad at working; like him that lay in the grass on a summer's day crying out, "O that this was what it was to work!" Solomon said, "The desire of the slothful kills him." How so? For "his hands refuse to labor;" he perishes in his desires. The believer joins desires and endeavors together. "One thing have I desired of the Lord, and that will I seek after."

3) A man's desires of grace may be unseasonable. Thus the foolish virgins desired oil when it was too late. The believer's desires are seasonable. He desires grace in the season of grace and seeks in a time when it may be found. The wise man's heart knows both time and judgment. He knows his season and has wisdom to improve it. The silly sinner does all his works out of season. He sends away the seasons of grace and then desires grace when the season is over. The sinner does all too late. Esau desired the blessing when it was too late and, therefore, he lost it; whereas, had he come sooner, he would have obtained it. Most men are like Epimetheus: wise too late. They come when the market is done. When the shop is closed, then they have their oil to get. When they lie upon their death-beds, then they desire holy hearts.

4) Desires of grace in many are very inconstant and fleeting, like the "morning dew that quickly passes away", or like Jonah's gourd that springs up in a night. They do not have root in the heart and, therefore, quickly perish.

Now, if a man may desire grace but not for grace's sake; if desires may be without endeavors; if a man may desire grace when it is too late; if these desires may be merely fleeting and inconstant, then may a man desire grace and yet be but almost a Christian.

A man may tremble at the Word of God and yet be but almost a Christian, as Belshazzar did at the handwriting upon the wall.

OBJECTION. But is not that a note of sincerity and truth of grace, to tremble at the Word? Does not God say, "To him will I look, that is of a poor and contrite spirit, and trembles at My Word?"

ANSWER. There is a two-fold trembling:

1. *One is when the Word reveals the guilt of sin and the wrath of God that belongs to that guilt.* This, where conscience is awake, causes trembling and amazement. Thus, when Paul preached of righteousness and judgment, it is said that Felix trembled.

2. *There is a trembling which arises from a holy dread and reverence of the majesty of God speaking in His Word.* This is only found in true believers, and is that which keeps the soul low in its own eyes. Therefore, mark how the words run: "To him will I look that is of a poor and contrite spirit, and trembles at My Word." God does not make the promise to him that trembles at the Word, for the devils believe and tremble. The Word of God can make the proudest, stoutest sinner in the world to shake and tremble, but it is to the poor and contrite spirit that trembles. Where trembling is the fruit of a spirit broken for sin, and low in its own eyes, there will God look. Now, many tremble at the Word, but not from poverty of spirit, not from a heart broken for sin and low in its own eyes, not from a sense of the majesty and holiness of God; and, therefore, notwithstanding they tremble at the Word, they are but almost Christians.

A man may delight in the Word and ordinances of

God and yet be but almost a Christian. They take delight in approaching God. And it is said of that ground, that it "received the Word with joy", and yet it was but "stony ground."

OBJECTION. But is it not made a character of a godly man to delight in the Word of God? Does not David say, "He is a blessed man that delights in the law of the Lord!"

ANSWER. There is a delighting in the Word which flows from grace and is a proof of blessedness.

1. *He that delights in the Word because of its spirituality is a Christian indeed.* The more spiritual the ordinances are, the more a gracious heart delights in them.

2. *When the Word comes close to the conscience, rips up the heart, and reveals sin, and yet the soul delights in it, notwithstanding, this is a sign of grace.*

3. *When delight arises from that communion that is to be had with God there, that is from a principle of grace in the soul.*

But there may be a delight in the Word where there is no grace.

1) There are many who delight in the Word because of the eloquence of the preacher. They delight not so much in the truths delivered as in the dress in which they are delivered. Thus it is said of the prophet Ezekiel that he was to them as "a very lovely song of one that hath a pleasant voice."

2) There are many who delight to hear the Word who yet take no delight to do it. So God said of them, "They delight to hear My words, but they do them not."

Now, then, if a man may delight in the Word more

because of the eloquence of the preacher than because
of the spirituality of the matter; if he may delight to
hear the Word and yet not delight to do it, then he
may delight in the Word and yet be but almost a
Christian.

SECTION VIII. **A man may be a member of the
church of Christ, he may join himself to the people of
God, partake with them in all ordinances, and share of
all church privileges and yet be but almost a Christian.**
So the five foolish virgins joined themselves to the
wise and walked together. Many may be members of
the church of Christ and yet not be members of Christ,
the Head of the church. There was a mixed multitude
who came up with the church of Israel out of Egypt.
They joined themselves to the Israelites, owned their
God, left their own country, and yet were in heart
Egyptians, notwithstanding. "All are not Israel that are
of Israel."

The church in all ages has had unsound members.
Cain had communion with Abel; Ishmael dwelt in the
same house with Isaac; Judas was in fellowship with the
apostles; and so was Demas with the rest of the disciples. There will be some bran in the finest meal. The
drag-net of the gospel catches bad fish as well as good.
The tares and the wheat grow together, and it will be
so till the harvest.

God has a church where there are no members but
such as are true members of Christ, but it is in heaven.
It is the "church of the first-born." There are no hypocrites, no rotten, unsound professors, none but the
"spirits of just men made perfect." All is pure wheat
that God lays up in that bin. There the chaff is sepa-

rated to unquenchable fire.

But in the church on earth, the wheat and the chaff lie in the same heap together. The Samaritans will be near of kin to the Jews when they are in prosperity. So, while the church of God flourishes in the world, many will join it. They will seem Jews, though they are Samaritans, and seem saints, though they are no better than almost Christians.

SECTION IX. A man may have great hopes of heaven, great hopes of being saved, and yet be but almost a Christian.

Indeed, there is hope of heaven which is "the anchor of the soul sure and steadfast." It never miscarries and is known by four properties:

1. *It is a hope that purifies the heart and purges out sin.* "He that hath this hope purifies himself even as God is pure." That soul that truly hopes to enjoy God truly endeavors to be like God.

2. *It is a hope which fills the heart with gladness.* "We rejoice in hope of the glory of God."

3. *It is a hope that is founded on the promise.* As there can be no true faith without a promise, so not any true hope. Faith applies the promise and hope expects the fulfilling of the promise. Faith relies upon the truth of it and hope waits for the good of it. Faith gives interest and hope expects livery and seisin.

4, *It is a hope that is wrought by God Himself in the soul.* He is, therefore, called, "the God of hope," as being the Author as well as the Object of hope. Now, he that has this hope shall never miscarry. This is a right hope, the hope of the true believer, "Christ in you the hope of glory." But, then, as there is a true and sound hope, so there is a false and rotten hope; and this is much more common, as bastard pearls are more frequently worn than true pearls.

There is nothing more common, than to see men big with groundless hopes of heaven, as:

A man may have great hope that has no grace. You read of the "hope of hypocrites." The performance of duties is a proof of their hope. The foolish virgins would never have done what they did had they thought they should have been shut out after all. Many professors would not be at such pains in duties as they are if they did not hope for heaven. Hope is the great motive to action; despair cuts the sinews of all endeavors. That is one reason why the damned in hell cease acting toward an alteration of their state, because despair has taken hold of them. If there were any hope in hell, they would up and be doing there. So that there may be great hope where there is no grace. Experience proves this - formal professors are men of no grace, but yet men of great hopes. Nay, many times, you shall find that none fear more about their eternal condition than they who have most cause of hope; and none hope more than they who have most cause of fear. As interest in hope may sometimes be without hope, so hope in God may be without interest.

A man may hope in the mercy, goodness, and power of God without eyeing the promise. This is the hope of most. God is full of mercy and goodness and, therefore, willing to save. And He is infinite in power and, therefore, able to save. Why, therefore, should I not rest on Him?

Now it is presumption and, therefore, sin to hope in the mercy of God other than by eyeing the promise;

for the promise is the channel of mercy through which it is conveyed. All the blessedness the saints enjoy in heaven is no other than what is the fruit of promise relied on and hoped for here on earth. A man has no warrant to hope in God but by virtue of the promise.

A man may hope for heaven and yet not cleanse his heart nor depart from his secret sins. That hope of salvation that is not accompanied with heart-purification is a vain hope.

A man may hope for heaven and yet be doing the work of hell. He may hope for salvation and yet be working out his own damnation, and so perish in his confidences. This is the case of many. Like the waterman that looks one way and rows another, many have their eyes on heaven whose hearts are in the earth. They hope in God but choose Him not for a portion. They hope in God but do not love Him as the best good and, therefore, are likely to have no portion in Him, nor good by Him, but are likely to perish without Him, notwithstanding all their hopes. "What is the hope of the hypocrite, though he hath gained, when God takes away his soul?"

Now, then, if a man may have great hope of heaven that has no grace; if he may hope in mercy without eyeing the promise; if he may hope without heart-purifying; if he may hope for heaven and yet do the work of hell, surely, then, a man may have great hopes of heaven and yet be but almost a Christian.

SECTION X. A man may be under great and visible changes, and these wrought by the ministry of the Word, and yet be but almost a Christian.

It is said, "When Herod heard John Baptist, he did

many things, and heard him gladly." Saul was under a great change when he met the Lord's prophets; he turned prophet too. Nay, it is said, verse 9 of that chapter, that "God gave him another heart." Now, was not this a work of grace? And was not Saul here truly converted? One would think he was, but yet, indeed, he was not. For though it is said God gave him "another" heart, yet it is not said that God gave him a "new" heart. There is a great difference between another heart and a new heart. God gave him another heart to fit him for a ruler, but did not give him a new heart to make him a believer. Another heart may make another man, but it is a new heart that makes a new man.

Again, Simon Magus is a great proof of this truth. He was under a great and visible change. Of a sorcerer, he was turned to be a believer. He left his witchcrafts and sorceries and embraced the gospel. Was not this a great change? If the drunkard leaves his drunkenness, the swearer his oaths, the profane person his profaneness, they think this is a gracious change and their state is now good. Alas! Simon Magus not only left his sins but had a kind of conversion, for "he believed and was baptized."

OBJECTION. But is not that man who is changed a true Christian?

ANSWER. Not every change makes a man a Christian. Indeed, there is a change that makes whoever is under it a true Christian.

When a man's heart is so changed that it is renewed; when old things "are done away and all is become new"; when the new creature is wrought in the soul; when a man is "turned from darkness to light and from the power of Satan to God; when the mind is enlightened, the will renewed, the affections made heavenly, then a man is a Christian indeed.

But now you must know that every change is not this change, for:

There is a civil change, a moral change, as well as a spiritual and supernatural change.

Many men are changed in a moral sense and, one may say, they have become new men; but they are, in heart and nature, the same men still. They are not changed in a spiritual and supernatural sense and, therefore, it cannot be said of them that they have become new creatures.

Restraining grace may cause a moral change, but it is renewing grace that must cause a saving change. Now, many are under restraining grace and changed morally who are not under the power of saving grace and changed savingly.

There is an outward change as well as an inward change. The outward change is often without the inward, though the inward change is never without the outward. A man's heart cannot be sanctified without it influencing the life, but a man's life may be reformed and yet it never affects or influences the heart.

A man may be converted from a course of profaneness to a form of godliness, from a filthy conversation to a fair profession, and yet the heart is the same in one and the other. A rotten post may be gilt without and yet unsound within. It is common to have the outside of the cup and platter made clean and yet the inside foul and filthy.

Now, then, if a man may be changed morally and yet not spiritually, outwardly and yet not inwardly, from a course of profaneness to a lifeless form of godliness, then a man may be under great and visible changes and yet be no more than almost a Christian.

I do not speak this to discountenance any change short of that which is spiritual, but to awaken you to seek after that change which is more than moral. It is good to be outwardly renewed, but it is better to be inwardly renewed. I know how natural it is for men to take up with anything like a work of conversion, though it is not conversion, and, resting in that, they eternally perish.

Beloved, let me tell you, there is no change, no conversion, that can stead your souls in the day of judgment this side of that saving work which is wrought on the soul by the Spirit of God renewing you throughout. The sober man, without this change, shall as surely go to hell as the foolish drunkard. Morality and civility may commend us to men, but not to God. They are of no value in the procurement of an eternal salvation.

A man may go far in an outward change and yet not be one step nearer heaven than he who was never under any change. Nay, he may be, in some sense, further off. Christ said the Scribes and Pharisees were further from heaven with all their show of godliness than publicans and harlots in all their sin and uncleanness. Resting in a false work, a partial change, we neglect to seek after a true and saving change. There is nothing more common than to mistake our state and, by overweening thoughts, misjudge our condition and so perish in our own delusions. The world is full of those foolish builders who lay the foundation of their hopes of eternal salvation upon the sand.

Now, my brethren, would you not mistake the way to heaven and perish in a delusion? Would you not be found fools at last? For none are such fools as the spiritual fool, who is a fool in the great business of salvation. Would you not be fools for your souls and for eternity? Oh, then, labor after, and pray for, a thorough work of conversion! Beg God that He would make a saving change in your souls, that you may be altogether Christians. All other changes below this saving change, this heart-change, make us but almost Christians.

SECTION XI. A man may be very zealous in the matters of religion and yet be but almost a Christian.

Jehu not only served God and did what He commanded, but was very zealous in his service. "Come with me, and see my zeal for the Lord of hosts!" And yet, in all this, Jehu was a hypocrite. Joash was a great reformer in Jehoiada's time. It is said, "He did that which was right in the sight of the Lord all the days of Jehoiada the priest." But when Jehoiada died, Joash's zeal for God died with him and he became a wretch.

OBJECTION. But the apostle makes zeal to be a note of sound Christianity. It is good to be zealously affected in good things. Nay, it seems to be the non-such qualification for obtaining eternal life. "The kingdom of heaven suffereth violence, and the violent take it by force."

ANSWER. It is true, there is a zeal which is good and renders the soul highly acceptable to God, a zeal that never misses heaven and salvation. Now, this is a zeal which is a celestial fire, the true temper and heat of all the affections to God and Christ. It is a zeal wrought and kindled in the soul by the Spirit of God who first works it and then sets it to work. It is a zeal that has the Word of God for its guide, directing it in working both in regard of its object and end, manner and measure. It is a zeal that checks sin and forwards the heavenly life. It is a zeal that makes the glory of God its chief end, which swallows up all by-ends. "The zeal of Thy house hath eaten me up."

But now, all zeal is not this kind of zeal. There is a false zeal as well as a true. Every grace has its counterfeit. As there is fire which is true heavenly fire on the altar, so there is strange fire. Nadab and Abihu offered strange fire upon God's altar.

8 KINDS OF COUNTERFEIT ZEAL

There are several kinds of zeal, none of which are true and sound but false and counterfeit. I shall instance in eight particulars:

1. *There is a blind zeal, a zeal without knowledge.* "They have a zeal," said the apostle, "but not according to knowledge." Now, as knowledge without zeal is fruitless, so zeal without knowledge is dangerous. It is like wildfire in the hand of a fool, or like the devil in the man possessed who threw him sometimes into the fire, sometimes into the water.

The eye is the light of the body and the understanding is the light of the soul. Now, as the body without the light of the eye cannot go without stumbling, so the soul without the light of the mind cannot act without erring. Zeal without knowledge is like a dim light in a dark night that leads a traveller out of his way into the bogs and mire. This was the zeal of Paul while he was a Pharisee. "I was zealous towards God, as ye are all this day, and I persecuted this way unto the death." And again, "I verily thought with myself, I ought to do many things contrary to the name of Jesus of Nazareth." And, "Concerning zeal persecuting the church." Such a zeal was that in John, "They shall put you out of the synagogue", silence you; you shall not be suffered to preach; "yea, the time comes that whoever kills you will think that he doth God service." This is great zeal, but yet it is blind zeal; and that God abhors.

2. *There is a partial zeal;* in one thing, fire-hot; in another, key-cold; zealous in this thing and yet careless in another. Many are first-table Christians - zealous in the duties of the first table and yet neglectful of the second. Thus, the Pharisees were zealous in their Corban and yet unnatural to their parents, suffering them to starve and perish. Others are mindful of the second-table, but neglectful of the first; more for righteousness among men than for holiness towards God. But now, he whose religion ends with the first table, or begins with the second, is a fool in his profession; for he is but almost a Christian.

The woman who was for dividing the child was not the true mother, and he who is for dividing the commands is not a true believer.

Jehu was zealous against Ahab's house but not so against Jeroboam's calves. Many are zealous against sin of opinion who yet use no zeal against the sins of their conversation.

Now, we know that the sweat of the whole body is a sign of health; but the sweat of some one part only shows a distemper and, therefore, physicians reckon such a heat to be symptomatic. So, where zeal reaches to every command of God alike, that is a sign of a sound constitution of soul; but, where it is partial, where a man is hot in one part and cold in another, this is symptomatic of some inward spiritual distemper.

3. *There is a misplaced zeal fixed upon unsuitable and disproportionate objects.* Many are very zealous in trifling things that are not worth it, and trifling in the things that most require it; like the Pharisees who were diligent tithers of mint, anise, and cummin, but neglected the "weightier matters of the law, judgment, mercy, and faith." They had no zeal for these, though they were very hot for the other. Many are more zealous for a ceremony than for the substance of religion; more zealous for bowing at the name of Jesus than for conformity to the life of Jesus; more zealous for a holy vestment than for a holy life; more zealous for the inventions of men than for the institutions of Christ. This is a superstitious zeal, and usually found in men unconverted in whom grace never was wrought. Against such men, heathens will rise up in judgment. When was it that Paul was so "exceeding zealous of the traditions of his fathers," as he said? Only when he was in his wretched and unconverted state! As you may see in the next verses: "But, when it pleased God to call me by His grace, then I conferred not with flesh and blood." Paul had another kind of zeal then, actuated by other kinds of principles.

4. *There is a selfish zeal that has a man's own end for its motive.* Jehu was very zealous, but it was not so much for God as for the kingdom; not so much in obedience to the command as in design to step into the throne;

and, therefore, God threatens to punish him for that very thing He commands him to do: "I will avenge the blood of Jezreel upon the house of Jehu;" because he shed blood to gratify his lust, not to obey God. So Simeon and Levi pretended great zeal for circumcision. They seemed very zealous for the honor of God's ordinances when, in truth, their zeal was covetousness and revenge upon the Shechemites.

5. *There is an outside zeal.* Such was that of Scribes and Pharisees. They would not eat with unwashed hands, but yet would live in unseen sins. They would wash the cup often but the heart seldom; paint the outside but neglect the inside. Jehu was a mighty outside reformer, but he reformed nothing within; for he had a base heart under all. "Jehu took no heed to walk in the law of the Lord with all his heart." Though his fleece was fair, his liver was rotten. Our Lord Christ observed of the Pharisees, "They pray to be seen of men;" and fast, so "that they may appear to men to fast."

6. *There is a forensic zeal that runs out upon others;* like the candle in the lantern that sends all the heat out at the top; or, as the lewd woman Solomon mentions, whose "feet abide not in her own house."

Many are hot and high against the sins of others and yet cannot see the same in themselves; like the Lamiae that put on their spectacles when they went abroad, but pulled them off within doors.

It is easy to see faults in others and hard to see them in ourselves. Jehu was zealous against Baal and his priests because that was Ahab's sin, but not against the calves of Bethel because that was his own sin. This zeal is the true character of a hypocrite. His own gar-

den is overrun with weeds while he is busy in looking
over his neighbour's pale.

7. *There is a sinful zeal.* All the former may be called
sinful from some defect, but this I call sinful in a more
special notion because it is against the life and chief of
religion. It is a zeal against zeal that flies not at
profaneness, but at the very power of godliness; not at
error, but at truth; and is most hot against the most
spiritual and most important truths of the times.
Whence else are the sufferings of men for the truth
but from the spirit of zeal against the truth? This may
be called a devilish zeal; for, as there is the faith of devils, so there is the zeal of devils. "Therefore his rage is
great, because he knows his time is short."

8. *There is a scripture-less zeal that is not butted and
bounded by the Word, but by some base and low end.* Such
was Saul's zeal when God bid him destroy Amalek and
spare neither man nor beast; when, contrary to God's
command, he spared the best of the sheep and oxen
under pretence of zeal for God's sacrifice. Another
time, when he had no such command, then he slew
the Gibeonites "in zeal to the children of Israel and
Judah."

Many a man's zeal is greater then and there, when
and where he has the least warrant from God. The true
spirit of zeal is bounded by Scripture, for it is for God
and the concerns of His glory. God has no glory from
that zeal which has no Scripture warrant.

Now, then, if the zeal of a man in the things of God
may be only a blind zeal, a partial zeal, a misplaced
zeal, a selfish zeal, an outside zeal, a forensic zeal, a
sinful zeal, or a scripture-less zeal, then it is evident
that a man may be very zealous in the matters of reli-

gion and yet be but almost a Christian.

SECTION XII. A man may be much in prayer. He may pray often and pray much and yet be but almost a Christian. So did the Pharisees whom yet our Lord Christ rejected for hypocrites.

OBJECTION. But is not a praying-frame an argument of a sincere heart? Are not the saints of God called "the generation of them that seek the face of God?"

ANSWER. A man is not, therefore, a Christian because he is much in prayer. I grant that those prayers that are from the workings and sighings of God's Spirit in us, from sincere hearts lifted up to God, from a sense of our own emptiness and God's infinite fulness, that are suited to God's will, the great rule of prayer; that are for spiritual things more than temporal, that are accompanied with faith and dependence, such prayers speak a man altogether a Christian. But, now, a man may be much in prayer and yet be a stranger to such prayer, as:

1. *Nature may put a man upon prayer, for it is a part of natural worship.* It may put a child of God upon prayer. So did Christ: "He went and fell upon His face, and prayed, saying, O My Father! if it be possible, let this cup pass from Me." This was a prayer of Christ which flowed from the sinless strugglings of nature seeking its own preservation.

2. *A man may pray in pretence for a covering to some sin.* So did those devout Pharisees: "Woe to you, Scribes and Pharisees, hypocrites! for ye devour widows' houses, and for a pretence make long prayer: therefore

ye shall receive the greater damnation." So the Papists seem very devout to pray a rich man's soul out of purgatory, but it is to cheat the heir of much of his estate under pretence of paying for his father's soul.

3. *A man may pray and yet love sin.* Austin, before conversion, prayed against his sin, but was afraid God should hear him and take him at his word. Now, God does not hear such prayers: "If I regard iniquity in my heart, God will not hear my prayer."

4. *A man may pray much for temporal things, and little for spiritual things; and such are the prayers of most men crying out most for temporal things.* More for, "who will show us any good?" than for, "Lord, lift upon us the light of Thy countenance." David copies out the prayer of such: "That our sons may be as plants, and that our daughters may be as corner-stones, polished after the similitude of a palace; that our garners may be full, etc. Happy is the people that is in such a case!" This is the carnal prayer, and this David calls vanity: "They are strange children whose mouth speaketh vanity."

5. *A man may pray and yet be far from God in prayer:* "This people draw nigh to Me with their mouth, and honor Me with their lips, but their heart is far from Me." A man may pray and yet have no heart in prayer; and that God chiefly looks at: "My son, give Me thy heart."

The Jews have this sentence written upon the walls of their synagogues: "Prayer, without the intention of the mind, is but a body without a soul."

It is not enough to be conscionable to use prayer, but we must be conscionable to the use of prayer. Many are so conscientious that they dare not but pray; and yet are so irreligious that they have no heart in prayer. A common work of God may make a man conscionable to do duties, but nothing less than Divine grace in the heart will make a man conscionable in the doing of them.

6. *A man's prayer may be a lie.* As a profession without sanctity is a lie to the world, so prayer without sincerity is a lie to God. It is said of Israel that they "sought God, and inquired early after Him." They were much in prayer and God called all but a lie. "Nevertheless, they did flatter Him with their mouths, and they lied to Him with their tongues, for their heart was not with Him." David said, "Hearken to my prayer, that goeth not out of feigned lips."

7. *Affliction and the pressure of outward evils will make a man pray and pray much.* "When He slew them, then they sought Him, and returned, and inquired early after God." The heathen mariners called every man upon his God when in a storm; when they fear drowning, then they fell to praying, Jonah 1:5. Mariners are, for the most part, none of the devoutest, nor much addicted to prayer. They will swear twice when they pray once, and yet it is said, "they cry to the Lord in their trouble." Hence you have a proverb, "He who cannot pray, let him go to the sea." They poured out a prayer when the chastening was upon them.

Now, then, if nature may put a man upon prayer; if a man may pray in pretence and design; if a man may pray and yet love sin; if a man may pray mostly for temporal things; if a man may pray and yet be far from God in prayer; if prayer may be a lie or only the cry of the soul under affliction; surely, then, a man may be much in prayer and yet be but almost a Christian.

OBJECTION. But suppose a man prays and prevails with God in prayer, surely that is a witness from heaven of a man's sincerity in prayer. I pray and prevail. I ask and am answered.

ANSWER. A man may pray and be answered, for God, many times, answers prayers in judgment. As God is sometimes silent in mercy, so He speaks in wrath. As He sometimes denies prayer in mercy, so He sometimes answers in judgment. When men are over-importunate in something their lusts are upon and will take no "nay," then God answers in judgment. "He gave them their own desire." They desired quails and God sent them; but, now, mark the judgment: "While the meat was in their mouths, the wrath of God came upon them, and slew them."

OBJECTION. But suppose a man's affections are much stirred in prayer. What then? Is that not a true note of Christianity? My affections are much stirred in prayer.

ANSWER. So were Esau's when he sought the blessing. "He sought it carefully with tears." A man may be affected with his own parts in a duty while good notions pass through his head and good words through his lips. Some good notions also may stir in his heart, but they are but sparks which fly out at the tunnel of the chimney which suddenly vanish. So that it is possible that a man may pray and prevail in prayer, pray and be affected in prayer, and yet be but almost a Christian.

SECTION XIII. A man may suffer for Christ in his goods, in his name, and in his person, and yet be but almost a Christian. Every man that bears Christ's cross on his shoulders does not, therefore, bear Christ's image in his soul.

OBJECTION. But does not our Lord Christ make great promises to those who suffer or lose any thing for Him? Does He not say, "Every one that hath forsaken houses, or brethren, or sisters, or father, or mother, or wife, or children, or lands, for My name's sake, shall receive an hundred fold, and shall inherit everlasting life?" Surely, they are true Christians to whom Christ makes this promise!

ANSWER. There is a suffering for Christ that is a note of sincerity and shall have its reward. That is, when a man suffers for a good cause, upon a good call, and with a good conscience, for Christ's sake and in Christ's strength; when His sufferings are a filling up "that which is behind of the sufferings of Christ"; when a man suffers as a Christian, "let him not be ashamed"; when a man thrusts not himself into sufferings, but stays God's call, such suffering is a proof of integrity.

But now, every suffering for Christ is not suffering as a Christian, for:

A man may suffer for Christ, for that profession of religion that is upon him. The world hates the show of religion. Times may come that it may cost a man as dearly to wear the livery of Christ as to wear Christ Himself. Alexander, as is generally judged, afterwards made shipwreck of faith and greatly opposed Paul's ministry.

A man may suffer for Christ and yet have no true

love to Christ. This is supposed: "Though I give my body to be burned, and have not charity, it profits nothing."

Love to Christ is the only noble ground of suffering, but a man may suffer much upon other ends:

1. Out of opinion of meriting by our sufferings, as the Papists; or,

2. Out of vain glory, or for applause among professors. Some have died that their names might live; or,

3. Out of a Roman resolution or stoutness of spirit.

4. Out of a design of profit. Judas forsook all for Christ, hoping to mend his market by closing with Him; or,

5. Rather to maintain an opinion than for truth's propagation. Socrates died for maintaining that there was but one God; but whether he died rather for his own opinion than for God's sake, I think, is no hard matter to determine. Thus, a man may suffer for professing Christ and yet suffer upon wrong principles.

Now, then, if a man may suffer for Christ from the profession that is upon him, then a man may suffer for Christ and yet be but almost a Christian.

SECTION XIV. A man may be called of God, and embrace this call, and be but almost a Christian.

Judas is a famous instance of this truth. He was called by Christ Himself, and came at the call of Christ, and yet Judas was but almost a Christian.

OBJECTION. But is not being under the call of God a proof of our interest in the predestining love of God? Does not the apostle say, "Whom He predestinated, them He called?" Nay, does He not say in the next verse, "Whom He called, them He justified?" Nay, does not God call all whom He intends to save?

ANSWER. Though God calls all those that shall be saved, yet all shall not be saved whom God calls. Every man under the gospel is called of God in one sense or other, but yet every man under the gospel shall not, therefore, be saved, for "many are called, but few are chosen". There is a twofold call of God: internal and external.

There is an internal call of God. Now, this call is a special work of the Spirit, by the ministry of the Word, whereby a man is brought out of the state of nature into a state of grace, out of darkness into light, from being a vessel of wrath to be made an heir of life. I grant that whoever is under this call of God is called effectually and savingly to be a Christian indeed. "Every man that hath heard and learned of the Father cometh to Me."

There is a call of God which a man may have and yet not be this call. There is an external call of God which is by the ministry of the Word.

Now every man that lives under the preaching of the gospel is thus called. God calls every soul to repent and lay a sure foundation for heaven and salvation by the word you hear this day.

But, now, every man that is thus called is not, therefore, a Christian, for many under the call of God come to Christ but are not converted to Christ, having nothing of the grace and life of Christ. He who, when Christ sent out His servants to bid guests unto the marriage, came in at the call of Christ, but yet "had not on the wedding garment"; had none of the grace and righteousness of Jesus Christ.

Many who are under the call of the gospel come to Christ and yet, afterwards, fall away from Christ as Judas and Demas did. It is said, when Christ preached a doctrine that His disciples did not like, that "from that time many of His disciples went back, and walked no more with Him."

Now, then, if many are only under this external call of God; if many that come to Christ are not converted to Christ but fall away from Christ, then a man may be called of God and yet be but almost a Christian.

SECTION XV. A man may have the Spirit of God and yet be but almost a Christian.

Balaam had the Spirit of God given him when He blessed Israel. "Balaam saw Israel abiding in tents, and the Spirit of the Lord came upon him." Judas had the Spirit for, by the Spirit, he cast out devils. He was one of them that came to Christ and said, "Lord, even the devils are subject to us." Saul had the Spirit, "Behold, a company of prophets met him; and the Spirit of God came upon him, and he prophesied among them."

OBJECTION. But you will say, "Can a man have the Spirit of God and yet not be a Christian?" Indeed, the Scripture says, "If any man have not the Spirit of Christ, he is none of His"; but, surely, if any man has the Spirit of Christ, he is His!

ANSWER. There is a having the Spirit which is a sure mark of saintship: where the Spirit is an effectual prevailing principle of grace and sanctification, renewing and regenerating the heart; where the Spirit is a potent worker helping the soul's infirmities; where the Spirit is so as to abide forever. But, now, every man that has the Spirit does not have the Spirit in this manner, for:

1. *A man may have the Spirit only transiently, not abidingly.* The Spirit may be in a man and yet not dwell in a man. The Spirit is wherever He dwells, but He does not dwell wherever He is. He is in all, but dwells in saints only. The hypocrite may have the Spirit for a season, but not to abide in him forever.

2. *A man may have the Spirit and yet not be born of the Spirit.* Every true Christian is born of the Spirit. A hypocrite may have the gifts of the Spirit, but not the graces. The Spirit may be in him by the way of illumination but not by way of sanctification; by way of conviction but not by way of conversion. Though he may have much common grace for the good of others, yet he may have no special grace for the good of himself. Though his profession is spiritual, yet his state and condition may be carnal.

3. *A man may have the Spirit only as a Spirit of bondage.* Thus, many have the Spirit working only to bondage. The Spirit of bondage is an operation of the Holy Ghost, by the Law, convincing the conscience of sin and of the curse of the law, and working in the soul such an apprehension of the wrath of God as makes the thoughts of God a terror to Him.

The Spirit may be, and often is, without saving grace. This operation of the Spirit was in Cain and Judas. There are none who receive the Spirit of adoption without first receiving the spirit of bondage, yet many receive the spirit of bondage who never receive the Spirit of adoption.

4. *A man may have the Spirit of God working in him, and yet it may be resisted by him.* It is said of the Jews,

"They rebelled, and vexed his Holy Spirit"; and the same sin is charged upon their children: "Ye stiff-necked, and uncircumcised in heart, ye have always resisted the Holy Ghost; as your fathers did, so do ye." The hypocrite does not retain the Spirit long enough to come up to regeneration and adoption, but quenches the motion of it and, thereby, miscarries eternally.

5. *A man may have the Spirit and yet sin that unpardonable sin.* He may have the Holy Ghost; nay, no man can sin this sin against it but he that has some degree of it.

The true believer has so much of the Spirit, such a work of it in him, that he cannnot sin that sin. "He that is born of God sins not"; to wit, that "sin unto death," for that is meant. The carnal professing sinner can not sin that sin because he is carnal and sensual, having not the Spirit. A man must have some measure of the Spirit that sins this sin. So has the hypocrite. He is said to be a "partaker of the Holy Ghost", and he only is capable of sinning the sin against the Holy Ghost.

Now, then, if a man may have the Spirit transiently only, not abidingly; if a man may have the Spirit and yet not be born of the Spirit; if he may have the Spirit only as a spirit of bondage; if a man may have the Spirit working in him and yet it may be resisted by him; if a man may have the Spirit and yet sin that unpardonable sin against it; then, surely, a man may have the Spirit of God and yet be but almost a Christian.

SECTION XVI. A man may have faith and yet be but almost a Christian.

The stony ground, that is, those hearers set out by the stony ground, "for awhile believed." It is said that many believed in the name of Christ, yet Christ did not commit Himself to them. Though they trusted in Christ, yet Christ would not trust them. Why not? "Because He knew all men." He knew they were rotten at root, notwithstanding their new faith. A man may have all faith to remove mountains and yet be nothing.

OBJECTION. But how can this be, that a man may have faith and yet be but almost a Christian? Does not our Lord Christ promise life eternal and salvation to all that believe? Is not this the gospel that is to be preached to every creature, "He that believes shall be saved?"

ANSWER. Though it is true what our Lord Christ said, that "he that believes shall be saved", yet it is true that many believe that shall never be saved. Simon Magus believed. Yea, James said, "The devils believe and tremble." Now, none will say these shall be saved. As it is true what the apostle said, "All men have not faith"; so it is as true that there are some men who have faith who are no whit the better for their faith.

You must know, therefore, there is a two-fold faith:

Faith that is special and saving.

Faith that is common and not saving.

There is a saving faith. This is called "faith of the operation of God." It is a work of God's own Spirit in the soul. It is such a faith as rests and casts the soul wholly upon Christ for grace and glory, pardon and peace, sanctification and salvation. It is a united act of the whole soul, understanding, will, and affections, all concurring to unite the soul to an all-sufficient Redeemer. It is such a faith as purifies the heart and makes it clean. It influences and gives strength and life

to all other graces. Now, whoever has this faith is a
Christian indeed. This is the faith of God's elect. But
then,

There is a common faith which is not saving, a fading and temporary faith. There is the faith of Simon
Magus as well as the faith of Simon Peter. Simon
Magus believed and yet he was in the "gall of bitterness
and the bond of iniquity." Now, the faith of most men
will at last be found to be no better than the faith of
Simon Magus, for:

1. *The faith of most is but a temporary faith.* It endures
for a while and then dies and perishes. True saving
faith, such as is the faith of God's elect, cannot die. It
may fail in the act but not in the habit. The sap may
not be in the branch but it is always in the root. That
faith that perishes, a man may have and perish.

2. *There is a faith that lies only in generals, not in
particulars.* As there is a general and particular object
of faith, so there is a general and particular faith. The
general object of faith is the whole Scripture; the particular object of faith is Christ in the promise. Now,
many have a general faith to believe all the Scripture
and yet have no faith to make particular application of
Jesus Christ in the promise. Devils and reprobates may
believe the truth of the Scripture and what is written of
the dying and suffering of Christ for sinners, but there
are but few that can close up themselves in the wounds
of Christ and, by His stripes, fetch in healing to their
own souls.

3. *There is a faith that is seated in the understanding but
not in the will.* This is a very common faith. Many assent
to the truth. They believe all the attributes of God, that
He is just, holy, wise, faithful, good, merciful. etc., but

yet they do not rest on Him, notwithstanding. They believe the commands are true but do not obey them. They believe the promises are true but do not embrace and apply them. They believe the threatenings are true but do not flee from them.

Thus their faith lies in assent but not consent. They have faith to confess a judgment but none to take out execution. By assent they lay a foundation, but never build upon it by application. They believe that Christ died to save them that believe and yet they believe not in Christ that they may be saved.

Oh, my brethren, it is not a believing head but a believing heart that makes a Christian: "with the heart man believes to righteousness." Without this, our faith is vain and we are yet in our sins.

4. *There is a faith without experience.* Many believe the Word, upon hearsay, to be the Word of God, but they have never felt the power and virtue of it upon their hearts and consciences. Now, what good is it to believe the truth of the Word if a man's conscience never felt the power of the Word? What is it to believe the truth of the promise if we have never tasted the sweetness of the promise? We are, in this case, like a man who believes the description others make of strange countries, but has never travelled there to know the truth; or like a patient who believes all the physician says but does not try any of his potions. We believe the Word because we cannot gainsay it, but yet we have no experience of any saving good wrought by the Word and so are but almost Christians.

5. *There is a faith that is without brokenness of heart, that does not avail to melt or soften the heart, and, therefore, is not true faith;* for the least true faith is ever joined with a

bending will and broken heart.

6. *There is a faith that does not transform the heart;* faith without fruit that does not bring forth the new creature in the soul, but leaves it in a state of sin and death. This is a faith that makes a man a sound professor but not a sound believer. He believes the truth but not as it is in Jesus, for then it would change and transform him into the likeness of Jesus. He believes that a man must be changed who would be saved, but yet is not savingly changed by believing. Thus, while others believe to salvation, he believes to damnation, for "his web shall not become a garment; neither shall he cover himself with his work."

Now, then, if a man's faith may be but temporary, or may lie only in generals; or may be seated in the understanding only; or may be without experience; or may be without a broken heart or without a new heart; surely, then, a man may have faith, he may taste of this "heavenly gift" and yet be but almost a Christian.

SECTION XVII. A man may go further yet. He may possibly have a love to the people of God and yet be but almost a Christian.

Every kind of love to those who are saints is not a proof of our saintship. Pharaoh loved Joseph and advanced him to the second place in the kingdom, yet Pharaoh was a wicked man. Ahab loved Jehoshaphat, made a league with him, and married his daughter Athaliah to Jehoram, Jehoshaphat's son. Yet Ahab was a wicked wretch.

OBJECTION. But, you will say, this seems to contradict the testimony of the Scripture, for that makes love to the saints and people of God a sure proof of our regeneration and interest in life eternal. "We know that we have passed from death to life, because we love the brethren." Nay, the Spirit of God puts this as a characteristic distinction between saints and sinners. "In this the children of God are manifest, and the children of the devil; whosoever doth not righteousness, is not of God, neither he that loveth not his brother." By brethren we do not understand brethren by place, those who are of the same country or nation, such as are called brethren in Romans 9:3 or Acts 7:23, 25. Nor do we understand brethren by race, those who are descended of the same parents; such are called brethren in James 1:2. But, by brethren, we understand brethren by grace and supernatural regeneration, such as are the children of God. These are the brethren whom to love is a sure sign that we are the children of God.

ANSWER. To this I answer that there is a love to the children of God which is a proof of our being the children of God. For instance, when we love them for that very reason, as being the saints of God; when we love them for the image of God which appears in them, because of that grace and holiness which shines forth in their conversation. This is truly commendable, to love the godly for godliness sake, the saints for saintship. This is a sure testimony of our Christianity. The love of grace in another is a good proof of the life of grace in ourselves. There can be no better evidence of the Spirit of Christ in us than to love the image of Christ in others. For this is a certain truth, a sinner cannot love a saint as such. "An Israelite is an abomination to an Egyptian." There is a contrariety and natural enmity between the two seeds, between the children of the world and those whom the Father in His eternal love has chosen out of the world.

It is likeness which is the great ground of love. Now, there is the highest dissimilitude and unlikeness between an unregenerate sinner and a child of God. He cannot love a sinner as a sinner: "In whose eyes a vile person is condemned." He may love him as a creature; he may love his soul, or he may love him under some relation that he stands in to him. Thus, God loves the damned spirits as they are His creatures; but, as fallen angels, He hates them with an infinite hatred. So, to love a sinner *quatenus* a sinner, this a child of God cannot do. So, neither can a sinner love a child of God as a child of God, that I grant; but it is upon some other consideration. He may love a person who is holy; not the person for his holiness, but for some other respect.

1. *A man may love a child of God for his loving, peaceable, courteous deportment to all with whom he converses.* Religion beautifies the conversation of a man and sets him off to the eye of the world. The grace of God is no friend to morose, churlish, unmannerly behavior among men. It promotes an affable demeanor and sweetness to all and, where this is found, it wins respect and love from all.

2. *A man may love a saint for his outward greatness and splendor in the world.* Men are very apt to honor worldly greatness and, therefore, the rich saint shall be loved and honored while the poor saint is hated and despised. This is as if a man should value the goodness of his sword by the embroidery of his belt, or his horse for the beauty of his trappings rather than for his strength and swiftness.

True love to the children of God reaches to all the children of God, poor as well as rich, bond as well as free, ignoble as well as noble; for the image of Christ is equally amiable and lovely in all.

3. *A man may love a child of God for his fidelity and usefulness in his place.* Where religion, in the power of it, takes hold of a man's heart, it makes him true to all his trusts, diligent in his business, faithful in all his relations, and this obliges respect. A carnal master may prize a goodly apprentice or servant that makes a conscience of pleasing his master and is diligent in promoting his interest.

I might instance in many things of the like nature, as charity, beauty, wit, learning, parts, etc., which may procure love to the people of God from the men of the world. But this love is no proof of charity, for:

It is but a natural love arising from some carnal respect or self-ends. That love which is made by the Scripture an evidence of our regeneration is a spiritual love, the principal loadstone and attractiveness whereof is grace and holiness. It is a love which embraces "a righteous man in the name of a righteous man."

A carnal man's love to saints is a limited and bounded love. It is not universal "to the seed." Now, as in sin, he that does not make conscience of every sin makes conscience of no sin as sin: so, he who does not love all in whom the image of Christ is found loves none for that of the image of Christ which is found in them.

Now, then, if the love we bear to the people of God may possibly arise from natural love only, or from some carnal respect; or, if it is a limited love, not extended to all the people of God, then it is possible that a man may love the people of God and yet be no better than almost a Christian.

SECTION XVIII. A man may obey the commands of God, yea, many of the commands of God, and yet be but almost a Christian.

Balaam seems very conscientious of steering his course by the compass of God's command. When Balak sent to him to come and curse the people of God, Balaam said, "If Balak would give me his house full of silver and gold, I cannot go beyond the word of the Lord my God." So he said, "The word that God putteth in my mouth, that shall I speak." The rich young man went far in obedience: "All these have I observed from my youth up," and yet he was but a hypocrite, for he forsook Christ after all.

OBJECTION. But is it not said, "He that hath My commandments, and keepeth them, he it is that loveth Me; and he that loveth Me shall be loved of My Father; and I will love him, and manifest Myself unto him?" And does not our Lord Christ tell us expressly, "Ye are My friends if ye do whatsoever I command you?" And can a man be a friend of Christ and be but almost a Christian?

I answer, there is an obedience to the commands of Christ which is a sure proof of our Christianity and friendship to Christ.

This obedience has a threefold property: 1. Evangelical; 2. Universal; and 3. Continual.

First, it is evangelical obedience both in the matter and manner, the ground and end.

In the matter of it; and that is what God requires;

"Ye are my friends if ye do whatsoever I command you."

In the manner of it; and that is according as God requires: "God is a Spirit; and they that worship Him must worship Him in spirit and in truth."

In the ground of it; and that is, "a pure heart, a good conscience, and a faith unfeigned."

In the end of it; and that is the honor and glory of God: "Whatsoever ye do, do all to the glory of God."

Second, it is a universal obedience which extends itself to all the commands of God alike. It respects the duties of both tables. Such was the obedience of Caleb, "who followed the Lord fully;" and of David who had "respect to all His commands."

Third, it is a continual obedience, putting the hand to God's plow without looking back. "I have inclined my heart to perform Thy statutes always, even to the end." He that thus obeys the command of God is a Christian indeed, a friend of Christ indeed. But all obedience to the commands of God is not this obedience, for:

There is a partial obedience, a piece-meal religion; when a man obeys God in one command and not in another; when a man seems to make conscience of the duties of one table and not of the duties of the other. This is the religion of most.

Now, this obedience is no obedience; for, as he that does not love God above all does not love God at all, so he that does not obey all the commands universally cannot be said to obey any command truly. It is said of those in Samaria that "they feared the Lord, and served their own gods after their own manner;" and yet, in the very next verse it is said, "They feared not the Lord." Their fear of the Lord was no fear. In like manner, that obedience to God is no obedience which is but a partial and piece-meal obedience.

A man may obey much and yet be in his old nature; and, if so, then all his obedience in that estate is but a painted sin. "He that offereth an oblation is as if he offered swine's blood; and he that burneth incense as if he blessed an idol." The nature must be renewed before the command can be rightly obeyed, "for a corrupt tree cannot bring forth good fruit". Whatever a man's performances are, they cannot be called obedience while the heart remains unregenerate because the principle is false and unsound. Every duty done by a believer is accepted of God as part of his obedience to the will of God, though it is done in much weakness; because, though the believer's hand is weak, yet "his heart is right." The hypocrite may have the most active hand, but the believer has the most faithful and sincere heart.

A man may obey the law and yet have no love to the Lawgiver. A carnal heart may do the command of God, but he cannot love God and, therefore, cannot do it right; for love to God is the foundation and spring of all true obedience. Every command of God is to be done in love. This is the "fulfilling of the law." The Apostle said, "Though I bestow all my goods to feed the poor, and though I give my body to be burned (these seem to be acts of the highest obedience), yet if I have not love, it profits me nothing."

I might add that a man may be much in obedience from sinister and base selfish ends. The Pharisees prayed much, gave much alms, fasted much, but our Lord Christ tells us that it was "that they might be seen of men, and have glory of men." Most of the hyp-

ocrite's piety empties itself into vainglory and, therefore, he is but an empty vine in all he does because "he
bringeth forth fruit to himself." It is the end that justi-
fies the action. Indeed, a good end cannot make a bad
action good, but the lack of a good end makes a good
action bad.

Now, then, if a man may obey the commands of
God partially and by halves; if he may do it and yet be
in his natural state, if he may obey the commands of
God and yet not love God, if the ends of his obedience
may be sinful and unwarrantable; then a man may be
much in obeying the commands of God and yet be but
almost a Christian.

**SECTION XIX. A man may be sanctified and yet be
but almost a Christian.**

Every kind of sanctification does not make a man a
new creature, for many are sanctified who are never
renewed. You read of those who "count the blood of
the covenant, wherewith they were sanctified, an unholy thing."

OBJECTION. But does not the Scripture tell us
that "both He that sanctifieth, and they who are sanctified, are all one; for which cause he is not ashamed to
call them brethren?" And can a man be one with
Christ and yet be but almost a Christian?

ANSWER. To this I answer, you must know there is
a two-fold work of sanctification spoken of in Scripture.
One is common and ineffectual, the other is special
and effectual.

That work of sanctification which is true and effectual is the working of the Spirit of God in the soul, en-

abling it to the mortifying of all sin, to the obeying of
every command, "to walking with God in all well-pleas-
ing." Now, whoever is thus sanctified is one with Him
that sanctifies. Christ will not be ashamed to call such
brethren, for they are "flesh of his flesh, and bone of
his bone."

But, then, there is a more common work of sanctification which is ineffectual as to the two great works of
dying to sin and living to God. This kind of sanctification may help to restrain sin but not to mortify sin. It
may lop off the boughs but it does not lay the axe to
the root of the trees. It sweeps and garnishes the room
with common virtues but does not adorn it with saving
graces, so that a man is but almost a Christian, notwithstanding this sanctification.

Or thus, there is an inward and outward sanctification. Inward sanctification is that which deals with the
soul and its faculties, understanding, conscience, will,
memory, and affections. Outward sanctification is that
which deals with the life and conversation. Both these
must concur to make a man a Christian indeed.
Therefore, the apostle puts them together in his prayer
for the Thessalonians: "The God of peace sanctify you
wholly! and I pray God, your whole spirit, and soul,
and body be preserved blameless unto the coming of
our Lord Jesus Christ." A man is then sactified wholly
when he is sanctified both inwardly and outwardly,
both in heart and affections and in life and conversation. Outward sanctification is not enough without inward, nor inward without outward. We must have both
"clean hands and a pure heart." The heart must be
pure that we may not incur blame from within and the
hands must be clean that we may not incur shame

from without. We must have hearts "sprinkled from an
evil conscience and bodies washed with pure water."
We must "cleanse ourselves from all filthiness of flesh
and spirit." Inward purity is the most excellent but,
without the outward, it is not sufficient. The true
Christian is made up of both.

Now, many have clean hands but unclean hearts.
They wash the outside of the cup and platter when all
is filthy within. Now, the former without the latter profits a man no more than it profited Pilate who condemned Christ to wash his hands in the presence of
the people. He washed his hands of the blood of Christ
and yet had a hand in the death of Christ. The
Egyptian temples were beautiful on the outside but
within you shall find nothing but serpents or
crocodiles. "He is not a Jew who is one outwardly."
Judas was a saint without but a sinner within; openly a
disciple but secretly a devil.

Some pretend to inward sanctity without outward.
This is the pretence of the open sinner. "Though I
sometimes drop an idle, foolish word," he says, "or
though I sometimes swear an oath, yet I think no hurt.
I thank God, my heart is as good as the best!" Such are
like the sinner Moses mentions who blessed himself in
his heart saying, "I shall have peace though I walk in
the imagination of mine own heart, to add drunkenness to thirst."

Some pretend to outward sanctity without inward.
Such are like the Scribes and Pharisees who "outwardly
appear righteous unto men, but within are full of
hypocrisy and iniquity"; fair professors but foul sinners.

Inward sanctity without outward is impossible, for it
will not reform the life. Outward sanctity without in-

ward is unprofitable for it will not reform the heart. A man is not a true Christian without both. The body does not make a man without the soul, nor the soul without the body; both are essential to the being of man. So the sanctification of both is essential to the being of the new man. True sanctification begins at the heart, but works out into the life and conversation; and yet, for lack of an inward, a man is no better than an almost Christian.

And so I shall end this long pursuit of the almost Christian in his progress heavenward with this one general conclusion:

SECTION XX. A man may do all as to external duties and worship that a true Christian can and, when he has done all, be but almost a Christian.

You must know that all the commands of God have an *intra* and an *extra*. There is the body and soul of the command. Accordingly, there is an internal and an external worship of God.

Now, the internal acts of worshipping of God are to love God, to fear God, to delight in God, to trust in God, etc.

The external acts of worshipping of God are by praying, teaching, hearing, etc.

Now, there is a vast difference between these internal and external acts of worship. There is such a difference that they distinguish the *altogether* from the *almost* Christian; the sincere believer from the unsound professor. Indeed, in this very thing the main difference between them lies.

1. *Internal acts of worship are good.* The goodness adheres intrinsically to the thing done. A man cannot

love God, nor fear God, but it will be imputed to Him as a gracious act and a great part of His holiness. But now, external acts of worship are not denominated good so much from the matter done, *propter fieri,* as from the manner of doing them. A man cannot sin in loving and delighting in God, but he may sin in praying and hearing, etc., for lack of a due manner.

2. *Internal acts of worship put a goodness into external.* It is our faith, our love, and our fear of God, that makes our duties good.

3. *They better the heart and magnify the degrees of a man's holiness.* External duties do not always do this. A man may pray and yet his heart never be the holier. He may hear the Word and yet his heart never be the softer; but now the more a man fears God, the wiser he is. The more a man loves God, the holier he is. Love is the perfection of holiness; we shall never be perfect in holiness until we come to be perfect in love.

4. *There is such an excellency in this internal worship that he who mixes it with his external duties is a true Christian when he does least; but, without this mixture, he is but almost a Christian that does most.*

Internal acts of worship, joined with outward, sanctify them and make them accepted of God though they are few. External acts of worship, without inward, make them abhorred of God though they are never so many. The almost Christian may do all those duties in hypocrisy which a true Christian does in sincerity. Nay, in doing external duties, he may out-do the true Christian like the comet makes a greater blaze than the true star. If Elijah fasts and mourns, Baal's priests will cut their flesh. Yet, the almost Christian cannot do those internal duties that the lowest true Christian can.

The almost Christian can pray but he cannot love God. He can teach or hear but he cannot take delight in God. Mark Job's query concerning the hypocrite: "Will he delight himself in the Almighty?" Will he take pleasure in God? Ah, no! He will not, he cannot! Delight in God arises from a suitableness between the faculty and the object. Now, none is more unsuitable than God and a carnal heart. Delight arises from having what we desire and from enjoying what we have. How, then, can he delight in God who neither enjoys, nor has, nor truly desires God? Delight in God is one of the highest exercises of grace. Therefore, how can he delight in God who has no grace?

Why, then, should any saint of God be discouraged when he hears how far the almost Christian may go in the way to heaven? Whereas, he who is the weakest true believer, who has the least true grace, goes further than he, for he believes in and loves God.

Should the almost Christian do less as to matter of external duties; yet, if he had but the least true faith, the least sincerity of love to Christ, he would surely be saved. Should the true Christian do ten times more duties than he does, yet, had he not faith in Christ and love to Christ, he would surely be rejected.

Oh, therefore, let not any weak believer be discouraged, though hypocrites may out-do them and go beyond them in duty; for all *their* duties are done in hypocrisy, but your faith and love to God in duties is a proof of your sincerity!

I do not speak this to discourage any soul in the doing of duties, or to beat down outward performances, but to rectify the soul in the doing of them. As the apostle said, "Covet earnestly the best gifts; but yet I

show you a more excellent way"; so I say, covet the best
gifts. Covet much to be in duties, much in prayer,
much in hearing, etc., "but I will show you a more excellent way," and that is the way of faith and love. Pray
much, but then believe much too. Hear much, read
much, but then love God much too. Delight in the
Word and ordinances of God much, but then delight
in the God of ordinances more.

And, when you are most in duties, as to your use of
them, Oh, then, be sure to be above duties as to your
resting and dependence upon them! Would you be
Christians indeed, altogether Christians? Oh, then, be
much in the use and exercise of ordinances, but be
much more in faith and dependence upon Christ and
His righteousness. When your obedience is most to the
command, then let your faith be most upon the
promise. The professor rests in duties, and so is but
almost a Christian; but you must be sure to rest upon
the Lord Christ. This is the way to be altogether
Christians for, if you believe, then are you Abraham's
seed and heirs according to the promise. Thus, I have
answered the first query - How far may a man go in the
way to heaven and yet be but almost a Christian?

1.   He may have much knowledge.
2.   He may have great gifts.
3.   He may have a high profession.
4.   He may do much against sin.
5.   He may desire grace.
6.   He may tremble at the word.
7.   He may delight in the word.
8.   He may be a member of the church of Christ.
9.   He may have great hopes of heaven.

10.   He may be under great and visible changes.
11.   He may be very zealous in the matters of
       religion.
12.   He may be much in prayer.
13.   He may suffer for Christ.
14.   He may be called of God.
15.   He may, in some sense, have the Spirit of God.
16.   He may have some kind of faith.
17.   He may love the people of God.
18.   He may go far in obeying the commands of
       God.
19.   He may be, in some sense, sanctified.
20.   He may do all, as to external duties, that a true
       Christian can, and yet be no better than almost
       a Christian.

Question 2

Why is it that many men go so far that they come to be almost Christians?

First, it may be to answer the call of conscience. Though few men have grace, yet all men have conscience. Now observe, and you shall see how far conscience may go in this work.

1. *Conscience owns a God, and that this God must be worshipped and served by the creature.* We have many atheists in practice; such the apostle speak of: "They profess to know God, but in works they deny Him." But none can be atheists in judgment. Marcus Tullius Cicero, a heathen, could say, "No race is so uncouth so as not to acknowledge the divine." Now, there being such a light in conscience as to discover that there is a God, and that He must be worshipped by the help of further light, the light of the Word, a man may be enabled to do much in the ways of God and yet his heart be without a particle of grace.

2. *Know this, that natural conscience is capable of great improvements from the means of grace.* Sitting under the ordinances may exceedingly heighten the endowments of conscience. It may be much regulated though it is not at all renewed. It may be enlightened and convinced, yet never savingly converted and changed. You read in Hebrews 6:4 of some who were once enlightened, tasted of the heavenly gift, and were made partakers of the Holy Ghost. What work shall we call this? It could not be a saving work, a true change and con-

version of state for, notwithstanding this enlightening, tasting, and partaking, they are said to fall away, verse 6. Had it been a true grace, they could never have fallen away from that. A believer may fall but he cannot fall away. He may fall foully but he cannot fall finally, for underneath are the everlasting arms. His faith is established in the strength of that prayer of Christ that our faith fail not. Nay, He tells us expressly that it is eternal life which He gives from which we shall never perish.

This work, then, here spoken of cannot be any saving work because it is not an abiding work, for they that are under it are said to fall away from it. But though it is not a saving grace, yet it is a supernatural work. It is an improvement made by the Word upon the consciences of men through the power of the Spirit. Therefore, they are said to taste the good Word of God and to be made partakers of the Holy Ghost. They have not the Spirit abiding in them savingly, but striving with them and working upon them convincingly to the awakening and setting conscience to work. And conscience, thus stirred, may carry a man very far in religion and the duties of the gospel and yet be but a natural conscience.

A common work of the Spirit may stead a man very much in the duties of religion, though it must be a special work of the Spirit that steads a man to salvation. A man may have the assisting presence of the Spirit enabling him to preach and pray, and yet he may perish for lack of the renewing presence of the Spirit enabling him to believe. Judas had the former and yet perished for lack of the latter. He had the Spirit assisting him to cast out devils, but yet he had not the Spirit renewing him for he was cast out himself. Thus a man may have an improved conscience and yet be a stranger to a renewed conscience; and conscience, thus improved, may put a man very much upon duty. I pray God none of us mistakes a conscience, thus improved by the Word, for a conscience renewed by the Spirit. The mistake is very easy, especially when a line of duties is the fruit of it.

3. *The conscience of a natural man is subject to distress and trouble.* Though a natural conscience is not sanctified with grace, yet it is often troubled at sin. Trouble of conscience is not incident to believers only, but sometimes to unbelievers also. A believer's conscience is sometimes troubled when his sin is truly pardoned; and a natural man's conscience is troubled for sin though it is never freed from sin. God sometimes sets the Word home upon the sinner's conscience and applies the terrors of the law to it, and this fills the soul with fear and horror of death and hell. Now, in this case, the soul usually betakes itself to a life of duties merely to fence trouble out of conscience.

When Absalom set Joab's corn fields on fire, then he ran to him though he refused before. So, when God lets a spark of hell, as it were, fall upon the sinner's conscience in applying the terrors of the Word, this drives the sinner to a life of duties which he never minded before. The ground of many a man's engaging in religion is the trouble of his conscience, and the end of his continuing in religion is the quieting of conscience. If conscience would never check him, God should never hear from him.

Natural conscience has a voice and speaks aloud, many times, in the sinner's ears and tells him, "This ought not to be done. God must not be forgotten. The commands of God ought not to be slighted. Living in sin will be the ruin of the soul." And hence it is that a natural man runs to duties and takes up a lifeless and graceless profession that he may thereby silence conscience. When a man is sick in his stomach, whatever sweet morsel he has eaten, he will bring up all. Although it was sweet in the eating, it is better in the rising. So it fares with the sinner when he is sermon-sick or conscience-sick. Though his sin was sweet in the practice, yet the thought of it rises bitter upon the conscience. And then his profession of religion is the pill he rolls about in his mouth to take away the bitterness of sin's taste.

4. *Natural conscience, enlightened by the Word, may reveal to a man much of the misery of a natural state;* though not effectually to bring him out of it, yet so as to make him restless and weary in it. It may show a sinner his nakedness and, hereupon, the soul runs to a life of duties, thinking hereby to stead the misery of his case and make a covering for his nakedness. It is said that when Adam and Eve "saw they were naked, they sewed fig-leaves together, and made themselves a covering." So, when once the sinner sees his nakedness and vileness by reason of sin, whereas he should run to Christ, close with Him, and beg His righteousness for a covering that the shame of his nakedness does not appear, he rather runs to a life of duty and performances; and thus makes himself a covering with the fig-leaves of a profession, without Christ truly embraced and conscience at all renewed. Natural man would fain be his own Saviour. He supposes a change of state to be a thing within his own power, and that the true work of

grace lies in leaving off the practice of sin and taking up a life of duties. Therefore, upon this principle, many a graceless professor outstrips a sound believer, for he rests on his own performances and hopes these will commend him to God.

Question 3

If a natural conscience may go thus far, then what difference is there between this natural conscience in hypocrites and sinners and a renewed conscience in believers? Or, how may I know whether the working of my conscience is the working of nature only or else of grace wrought in it?

ANSWER. I grant that it is difficult to distinguish between the one and the other, and the difficulty has a two-fold rise:

First, it arises from that hypocrisy that is in the best saints. The weakest believer is no hypocrite, but yet there is some hypocrisy in the strongest believer. Where there is most grace there is some sin, and where there is most sincerity there is some hypocrisy.

Now it is very incident to a tender conscience to misgive and mistrust its state upon the sight of any sin. When he sees hypocrisy break out in any duty or performance, then he complains, "Surely my aims are not sincere! My conscience is not renewed! It is but natural conscience enlightened, not by grace purged and changed." (Pygmalion made an image so lively that he deceived himself; and, taking the picture for a person, he fell in love with the picture.)

Second, it arises from that resemblance there is between grace and hypocrisy; for hypocrisy is a resemblance of grace without substance, the likeness of grace without the life of grace. There is no grace but a hypocrite may have something like it, and there is no duty done by a Christian but a hypocrite may outstrip him in it. Now, when one that does not have true grace shall go further than one that has, this may well make the believer question whether his grace is true or not; or whether the workings of his conscience are not the workings of nature only rather than of grace wrought in it.

MARKS OF A NATURAL CONSCIENCE

To answer the question, you may make a judgment of this in these seven particulars:

1. *If a natural man's conscience puts him upon duty, he usually bounds himself in the work of God.* His duties are limited; his obedience is a limited obedience. He does one duty and neglects another. He picks and chooses among the commands of God, obeys one and slights another. "This much is enough; why do I need any more? If I do this and this, I shall go to heaven at last." But now, where conscience is renewed by grace, it is otherwise. Though there may be many weaknesses which accompany its duties, yet that soul never bounds itself in working after God. It never loves God so much but still it would love Him more; nor seeks Him so much but still it would seek Him more; nor does it serve God so well at any time but it still makes conscience of serving Him better. A renewed conscience is a spring of universal obedience, for it sees an infinite excellency, goodness, and holiness in God and, therefore, would fain have its services rise up towards some proportionableness to the object. "A God of infinite excellency and goodness should have infinite love,"

says conscience. "A holy God should have service from a holy heart," says conscience.

Now, then, if I set bounds to my love to God, or to my service to God; if I limit myself in my obedience to the holy God, love one command and slight another; obey in one point and yet lie cross in another; then all I do is but the workings of a natural conscience. But, on the other hand, if I love the Lord with my whole heart and whole soul, and serve Him with all my might and strength; if "I esteem all God's precepts concerning all things to be right, and have respect to all His commands", then my love and service is from a renewed conscience.

2. *If a natural man's conscience checks or accuses for sin, then he seeks to stop the mouth of it but not to satisfy it.* Most of the natural man's duties are to still and stifle conscience. But now, the believer chooses rather to let conscience cry than to stop the mouth of it, until he can do it upon good terms and can fetch in satisfaction to it from the blood of Jesus Christ by fresh acts of faith apprehended and applied. The natural man seeks to still the noise of conscience rather than to remove the guilt. The believer seeks the removal of guilt by the application of Christ's blood and then conscience is quiet of itself. As a foolish man, having a mote fallen into his eye and making it water, wipes away the water and labors to keep it dry, but never searches his eye to get out the mote; but a wise man minds not so much the wiping as the searching his eye. Something has gotten in that caused the watering and, therefore, the cause must be removed. Now, then, if, when conscience accuses for sin, I take up a life of duties, a form of godliness, to stop the mouth of conscience; and if,

hereupon, conscience is still and quiet, then this is but a natural conscience. But if, when conscience checks, it will not be satisfied with anything but the blood of Christ and, therefore, I use duties to bring me to Christ; and if I beg the sprinkling of His blood upon conscience and labor not so much to stop the mouth of it as to remove guilt from it, then this is a renewed conscience.

3. *There is no natural man, let him go never so far, let him do never so much in the matters of religion, but still he has his Delilah, his bosom-lust.* Judas went far, but he carried his covetousness along with him. Herod went far; he did many things under the force of John's ministry, but yet there was one thing he did not do. He did not put away his brother's wife. His Herodias lay in his bosom still. Nay, commonly all the natural man's duties are to hide some sin. His profession is only made use of for a cover-shame. But, now, the renewed conscience hates all sin as David did. "I hate every false way." He regards no iniquity in his heart. He uses duties not to cover sin, but to help work down and work out sin. Now, then, if I profess religion; if I make mention of the name of the Lord and make my "boast of the law, and yet through breaking the law, dishonor God;" if I live in the love of any sin and make use of my profession to cover it, then I am a hypocrite and my duties flow but from a natural conscience. But, on the other hand, if I name the name of the Lord Jesus and depart from iniquity; if I use duties not to cover but to reveal and mortify sin, then am I upright before God and my duties flow from a renewed conscience.

4. *A natural man prides himself in his duties. If he is much in duty, then he is much lifted up under duty.* So did

the Pharisee, "God, I thank Thee that I am not as other
men are." And why? Where does the difference lie?
Why, "I fast twice a week; I give tithes of all. . . ."

But, now, take a gracious heart, a renewed conscience, and when his duties are highest, then his heart
is lowest. Thus it was with the apostle Paul. He was
much in service, "in season, and out of season",
preaching up the Lord Jesus with all boldness and
earnestness; and yet very humble, in a sense, of his own
unworthiness under all. "I am not worthy to be called
an apostle. To me, who am less than the least of all
saints, is this grace given, that I should preach among
the Gentiles the unsearchable riches of Christ." And
again, "Of sinners I am the chief." Thus a believer,
when he is highest in duties, then is he lowest in humility. Duty puffs up the hypocrite, but a believer
comes away humbled. Why? Because the hypocrite has
had no visions of God. He has seen only his own gifts
and parts, and this exalts him. But the believer has
seen God, and enjoyed communion with God, and this
humbles him. Communion with God, though it is very
refreshing, is also very abasing and humbling to the
creature. Jerome observes on Zephaniah 1:1, where it
is said that "Cushi was the son of Gedaliah, the son of
Amariah"; that "Amariah signifies the 'Word of the
Lord.' Gedaliah signifies 'the Greatness of the Lord,'
and Cushi is interpreted 'humility' or 'my Ethiopian.' "
"So that," said he, "from the Word of the Lord comes a
sight of the Greatness of the Lord; and from a sight of
the greatness of the Lord comes humility."

Now, then, if I pride myself in any duty and am
puffed up under my performances, then I have not
seen nor met with God in any duty. But, on the other

hand, if when my gifts are highest my heart is lowest; if
when my spirit is most raised my heart is most humbled; if, in the midst of all my services, I can maintain a
sense of my own unworthiness; if Cushi is the son of
Gedaliah, then I have seen and had communion with
God in duty and my performances are from a renewed
conscience.

5. *Look what that is to which the heart secretly renders the
glory of a duty, and that is the principle of the duty.* In
Habakkuk 1:16, we read of them that "sacrifice to their
net, and burn incense to their drag." Where the glory
of an action is rendered to a man's self, the principle
of that action is self. All rivers run into the sea; that is
an argument that they come from the sea. So, when all
a man's duties terminate in self, then self is the principle of all. Now, all the natural man's duties run into
himself. He was never, by a thorough work of grace,
truly cast out of himself and brought to deny himself;
and, therefore, he can rise no higher than himself in
all he does. He was never brought to be poor in spirit
and so to live upon another, to be carried out of all duties to Jesus Christ. But the believer gives the glory of
all his services to God. Whatever strength or life there
is in duty, God has all the glory; for he is, by grace, put
out of himself and, therefore, sees no excellence or
worthiness in self.

"I labored more abundantly than they all," said the
apostle; but to whom does he ascribe the glory of this?
To self? No! "Yet not I," said he, "but the grace of God
which was with me." Whenever the grace of Christ is
wrought in the heart as a principle of duty, you shall
find the soul, when it is most carried out, with a "Yet
not I" in the mouth of it. "I live, yet not I; I labored

more abundantly than all, yet not I." Self is disclaimed
and Christ most advanced when it is from grace that
the heart is quickened. The twenty-four elders cast
their crowns at Christ's feet.

There are two things very hard. One is to take the
shame of our sins to ourselves, the other is to give the
glory of our services to Christ. Now, then, if I sacrifice
to my own net, if I aim at my own credit or profit and
give the glory of all I do to self, then I "sow to the
flesh," and was never cast out of self, but act only from
a natural conscience. But, if I give the glory of all my
strength and life in duty only to God, if I magnify grace
in all and can truly say in all I do, "Yet not I", then I am
truly cast out of self and do what I do with a renewed
conscience.

6. *Though a natural conscience may put a man much
upon service, yet it never presses to the attainment of holiness.*
So he carries an unsanctified heart under all. How
long was Judas a professor, and yet he had not gotten
one particle of grace! The foolish virgins, you know,
"took their lamps, but took no oil in their vessels"; that
is, they looked more after a profession than after a
sanctification. But now, when a renewed conscience
puts a man upon duty, it is succeeded with the growth
of holiness. As grace helps to the doing of duty, so duty
helps to the growing of grace. A believer is the more
holy and the more heavenly by his being much in duties.

Now, then, if I am much in a life of duties and yet a
stranger to a life of holiness; if I maintain a high profession and yet have not a true work of sanctification;
if, like children in the rickets, I grow big in the head
but weak in the feet, then have I gifts and parts but no

grace. And, though I am much in service, yet I have
but a natural conscience. But, on the other hand, if the
holiness of my conversation carries a proportion to my
profession; if I am not a hearer of the Word only but a
doer of it; if grace grows in seasons of duty, then I act
in the things of God from a renewed conscience.

7. *And lastly, if a natural conscience is the spring of duty,
why, then, this spring runs fastest at first and so abates and,
at last, dries up.* But if a renewed conscience, a sanctified heart, is the spring of duty, then this spring will
never dry up. It will run always from first to last and
run quicker at last than first. "I know thy works, and
the last to be more than the first." The righteous shall
hold on his way, and he that has clean hands shall be
stronger and stronger.

QUESTION. But you will say, "Why does that man
abate and languish in his duties that does them from a
natural conscience more than he that does them from
a renewed conscience?"

ANSWER. The reason is because they grow upon a
fallible root, a decaying root, and that is nature. Nature
is a fading root, and so are all its fruits fading; but the
duties done by a renewed conscience are fruits that
grow upon a lasting root, and that is Christ. Gifts have
their root in nature, but grace has its root in Christ.
And, therefore, the weakest grace shall outlive the
greatest gifts and parts; because there is life in the root
of the one and not in that of the other. Gifts and grace
differ like the leather of your shoe and the skin of your
foot. Take a pair of shoes that have the thickest soles
and, if you walk much in them, the leather wears out
and, in a little time, a man's foot comes to the ground.

But, now, a man who goes barefoot all his days, the skin of his feet does not wear out. Why should not the sole of his foot sooner wear out than the sole of his shoe, for the leather is much thicker than the skin? The reason is because there is life in the one and not in the other. There is life in the skin of the foot and, therefore, that holds out and grows thicker and thicker, harder and harder; but there is no life in the sole of his shoe and, therefore, it wears out and waxes thinner and thinner. So it is with gifts and grace.

Now, then, if I decay, abate, grow weary of a profession, and fall away at last; if I begin in the spirit and end in the flesh, then all I did was from a natural conscience. But if I grow and hold out, if I persevere to the end, and my last works are more than my first, then I act from a renewed conscience.

And, thus, I have, in seven things, answered that question, namely, "If conscience may go thus far in putting a man upon duties, then what difference is there between this natural conscience in hypocrites and sinners, and renewed conscience in believers?"

And that is the first answer to the main query, namely, "How is it that many men go so far that they come to be almost Christians?" It is to answer the call of conscience.

Second, it is from the power of the Word under which they live. Though the Word does not work effectually upon all, yet it has a great power upon the hearts of sinners to reform them, though not to renew them.

1. *It has a discerning, discovering power.* "The Word of God is quick and powerful, sharper than any two-edged sword, piercing to the dividing asunder of soul and

spirit, and of the joints and marrow"; and is a discerner of the thoughts and intents of the heart. This is the glass wherein every one may see what man he is. As the light of the sun discovers the little motes, so the light of the Word, shining into conscience, discovers little sins.

2. *The Word has the power of a law.* It gives law to the whole soul and binds conscience. It is, therefore, frequently called "the Law" in Scripture. "Unless Thy law had been my delight," etc.' "to the Law, and to the testimony." This is spoken of the whole Word of God, which is, therefore, called a law because of its binding power upon the conscience.

3. *It has a judging power.* "The word that I have spoken, the same shall judge him at the last day." The sentence that God will pass upon sinners hereafter is no other than what the Word passes upon them here. The judgment of God is not a day wherein God will pass any new sentence, but it is such a day wherein God will make a solemn, public ratification of the judgment passed by the ministry of the Word upon souls here. This I gather clearly from Matthew 18:18, "Whatsoever ye shall bind on earth shall be bound in heaven; and whatsoever ye shall loose on earth shall be loosed in heaven;" so that, by bringing a man's heart to the Word and trying it by that, he may quickly know what that sentence is that God will pass upon his soul in the last day; for as the judgment of the Word is now, such will the judgment of God be concerning him in the last day.

Indeed, there is a two-fold power further than this in the Word. It has a begetting and saving power, but this is put forth only upon some. But the other is more extensive, and has a great causality upon a profession of goodness, even among them who have no grace.

A man who is under this three-fold power of discerning law and judgment, who has his heart ransacked and discovered, his conscience bound and awed, his state and sinful condition judged and condemned, may take up a resolution of a new life and convert himself to great profession of religion.

Third, a man may go far in this course of profession from affectation of applause and credit and to get a name in the world. As it is said of the Pharisees, they "love to pray in the market-places and in the corners of the streets, to be seen of men." Many are of Machiavel's principle: that the appearance of virtue is to be sought because, though the use of it is a trouble, yet the credit of it is help. Jerome, in his Epistle to Julian, calls such, "the base bond-slaves of common fame." Many a man does that for credit which he will not do for conscience; and owns religion more for the sake of lust than for the sake of Christ, thus making God's stream to turn the devil's mill.

Fourth, it is from a desire of salvation. There is, in all men, a desire of salvation. It is natural to every being to love and seek its own preservation. "Who will show us any good?" This is the language of nature, seeking happiness to itself.

Many a man may be carried so far out in the desires of salvation as to do many things to obtain it. So did the young man: "Good Master, what good thing shall I do that I may inherit eternal life?" He went far, and did much, obeying many commands, and all out of desire of salvation. So then, put these together and there is an answer to that question.

The call of conscience, the power of the Word, the affectation of credit, and the desire of salvation. These may carry a man so far as to be almost a Christian.

Question 4

How is it that many are but almost Christians when they have gone thus far? What is the cause of this?

ANSWER. I might multiply answers to this question, but I shall instance in only two which I judge the most material.

First, it is for lack of right and sound conviction. If a man is not thoroughly convinced of sin and his heart truly broken, whatever his profession of godliness may be, yet he will be sure to miscarry. Every work of conviction is not a thorough work; there are convictions that are only natural and rational, but not from the powerful work of the Spirit of God.

Rational conviction is that which proceeds from the working of a natural conscience, charging guilt from the light of nature by the help of those common principles of reason that are in all men. This is the conviction you read of in Romans 2:14-15. It is said that the Gentiles who did not have the law still had their consciences bearing witness and accusing or excusing one another. Though they did not have the light of Scripture, yet they had conviction from the light of nature. Now, by the help of the Gospel light, these convictions may be much improved and yet the heart not renewed.

But then there is a spiritual conviction, and this is that work of the Spirit of God upon the sinner's heart, by the Word, whereby the guilt and filth of sin is fully discovered and the woe and misery of a natual state distinctly set home upon the conscience to the dread and terror of the sinner while he abides in that state and condition. And this is the conviction that is a sound and thorough work. Many have their convictions, but not this spiritual conviction.

QUESTION. Now you will say, "Suppose I am at any time under conviction; how shall I know whether my convictions are only from a natural conscience or whether they are from the Spirit of God?"

ANSWER. I should digress too much to draw out the solution of this question to its just length. I shall, therefore, in five things only lay down the most considerable difference between the one and the other.

1. *Natural convictions reach chiefly to open and scandalous sins, sins against the light of nature, for natural conviction can reach no further than natural light.* But spiritual conviction reaches to secret, inward, and undiscerned sins such as hypocrisy, formality, lukewarmness, deadness, and hardness of heart, etc.

Observe, then, whether your trouble for sin looks inward as well as outward and reaches not only to open sins but to secret lusts; to inward and spiritual sins. And, if so, this is a sure sign of the work of the Spirit, because the trouble occasioned by these sins bears a more immediate relation to the holiness of God, who only is offended by them, they being such as none else can see or know.

2. *Natural convictions deal only with a man's conversation, not with his state and condition; with sins actual, not original.* But spiritual conviction reaches to all sins - to sins of heart as well as sins of life; to the sin of our nature as well as the sins of practice; to the sin that is

born in us as well as the sin that is done by us. Where the Spirit of the Lord comes to work effectually in any soul, He holds the glass of the law before the sinner's eyes, opens his eyes to look into the glass and see all that deformity and filthiness that is in his heart and nature.

The apostle Paul said, "I had not known sin but by the law." How can this be true, that he had not known sin but by law, when the light of nature reveals sin? It is said of the Gentiles that, not having the law, they were a law to themselves. This sin, therefore, that the apostle speaks of is not to be understood of sin actual but of sin original. "I had not known the pollution of nature, that fountain of sin that is within; this I had not known, but by the law." And, indeed, this is a discovery that natural light cannot make.

It is true, the philosopher could say that "lust is the first and chief of all sins." But I cannot think he meant it of original sins, but of the inordinacy of appetite and desire at most; for I find that the wisest of the philosophers understood nothing of original sin. Hear Seneca, "Sin is not born with you, but brought in since."

Quintilian said, "It is more marvel that any one man sins than that all men should live honestly; sin is so against the nature of men." How blind they were in this point! So was Paul till the Spirit of the Lord revealed it to him by the Word. And, indeed, this is a revelation proper to the Spirit. It is He that makes the sinner see all the deformity and filthiness that is within. It is He that pulls off all a sinner's rags and makes him see his naked and wretched condition. It is He that shows us the blindness of the mind, the stubborness of the will, the disorderedness of the affections, the searedness of the conscience, the plague of our hearts and the sin of our natures and, therein, the desperateness of our state.

3. *Natural convictions carry the soul out to look more on the evil that comes by sin than on the evil that is in sin.* So that the soul under this conviction is more troubled at the dread of hell, wrath, and damnation than at the vileness and heinous nature of sin. But, now, spiritual convictions work the soul into a greater sensibleness of the evil that is in sin than of the evil that comes by sin; the dishonor done to God by walking contrary to His will; the wounds that are made in the heart of Christ; the grief that the Holy Spirit of God is put to, this wounds the soul more than a thousand hells.

4. *Natural convictions are not durable; they are quickly worn out.* They are like a slight cut in the skin that bleeds a little and is sore for the present, but is soon healed again and, in a few days, not so much as a scar to be seen. But spiritual convictions are durable; they cannot be worn out. They abide in the soul till they have reached their end, which is the change of the sinner.

The convictions of the Spirit are like a deep wound in the flesh that goes to the bone and seems to endanger the life of the patient and is not healed but with great skill. When it is healed, it leaves a scar behind it that, when the patient is well, yet he can say, "Here is the mark of my wound which will never wear out." So a soul that is under spiritual conviction, his wound is deep and not to be healed but by the great skill of the heavenly Physician; and, when it is healed, there are the tokens of it remaining in the soul that can never be worn out. So that the soul may say, "Here are the marks and signs of my convictions still in my soul."

5. *Natural convictions make the soul shy of God. Guilt works fear and fear causes estrangedness.* Thus it was with Adam; when he saw his nakedness, he ran away and hid himself from God. Now, spiritual convictions do not drive the soul from God, but unto God. Ephraim's conviction was spiritual, and he ran to God. "Turn Thou me, and I shall be turned." So that there is, you see, a great difference between conviction and conversion; between that which is natural and that which is spiritual; that which is common and that which is saving. Yea, such is the difference that, though a man has never so much of the former, yet, if he is without the latter, he is but almost a Christian. And, therefore, we have great reason to inquire more after this spiritual conviction; for:

Spiritual conviction is an essential part of sound conversion. Conversion begins here. True conversion begins in convictions and true convictions end in conversion. Till the sinner is convinced *of* sin, he can never be converted *from* sin. Christ's coming was as a Saviour to die for sinners, and the Spirit's coming is to convince us as sinners that we may close with Christ as a Saviour. Till sin is thoroughly revealed to us, interest in the blood of Christ cannot rightly be claimed by us. Nay, as long as sin is unseen, Christ will be unsought. "They that be whole need not the physician, but they that are sick."

Slight and common convictions, when they are but skin deep, are the cause of much hypocrisy. Slight convictions may bring the soul to clasp about Christ but not to close with Christ, and this is the guise of a hypocrite. I know no other rise and spring of hypocrisy like this of slight convictions; this has filled the church of Christ with hypocrites. Nay, it is not only the spring of hypocrisy, but is also the spring of apostasy. What was the cause that the seed was said to wither away? It was because it had no deepness of earth. Where there is thorough conviction, there is a depth of earth in the heart and there the seed of the Word grows. But where convictions are slight and common, there the seed withers for lack of depth. So that you see clearly in this one instance why it is that many are but almost Christians, when they have gone so far in religion, to wit, for lack of sound convictions.

Second, and this has a near relation to the former, it is for lack of a thorough work of grace first wrought in the heart. Where this is not, all a man's following profession comes to nothing. That scholar is never likely to read well that will be in his grammar before he is out of his primer. Cloth that is not wrought well in the loom will never wear well nor wear long. It will do little service. That Christian who does not come well off the loom, who does not have a thorough work of grace in his heart, will never wear well. He will shrink in the wetting and never do much service for God. It is not the pruning of a bad tree that will make it bring forth good fruit, but the tree must be made good before the fruit can be good.

He who takes up a profession of religion with an unbroken heart will never serve Christ in that profession with his whole heart. If there is not a true change in that man's heart who yet goes far and does much in the ways of God, to be sure, he will either die a hypocrite or an apostate.

In nature, if a man is not well born, but proves to be crooked or misshapen in the birth, he will be crooked as long as he lives. You may bolster or stuff out his clothes to conceal it, but the crookedness, the deformity, remains still. You may hide it but you cannot help it. It may be covered but it cannot be cured. So it is in this case. If a man comes to a profession of religion but is not rightly born; if he is not "begotten of God and born of the Spirit"; if there is not a thorough work of grace in his heart, all his profession of religion will never mend him. He may be bolstered out by a life of duties, but he will be but a hypocrite at last for lack of a thorough work at first. A form of godliness may cover his crookedness but will never cure it.

A man can never be a true Christian nor accepted of God, though in the highest profession of religion, without a work of grace in the heart, for:

There must be an answerableness in the frame of that man's heart who would be accepted of God to the duties done by him. The spirit and affections within must carry a proportion to his profession without. Prayer without faith, obedience to the law given without fear and holy reverence of the Lawgiver, God abhors. Acts of internal worship must answer the duties of external worship. Now, where there is no grace wrought in the heart, there can never be any proportion or answerableness in the frame of that man's heart to the duties done by him.

Those duties that find acceptance with God must be done in sincerity. God does not take our duties by tale, nor judge us according to the frequency of our performances, but according to the sincerity of our hearts in the performance. It is this that commends both the doer and the duty to God. With sincerity, God accepts the least we do; without sincerity, God rejects the most we do or can do. This is that temper of spirit which God highly delights in: "They that are of a froward heart are an abomination to the Lord, but such as are upright in the way are his delight." The Apostle gives it a great epithet. He calls it in 2 Corinthians 1:12 "the sincerity of God"; that is, such a sincerity as is His special work upon the soul, setting the heart right and upright before Him in all his ways. This is the crown of all our graces and the commendation of all our duties. Thousands perish and go to hell in the midst of all their performances and duties merely for lack of a little sincerity of heart to God.

Now where there is not a change of state, a work of grace in the heart, there can be no sincerity to God, for this is not an herb that grows in nature's garden. "The heart of man is naturally deceitful and desperately wicked"; more opposite to sincerity than to anything; as things corrupted carry a greater dissimilitude to what they were than to anything else which they never were.

"God made man upright." Now man, voluntarily losing this, has become more unlike himself than anything below himself. He is more like a lion, a wolf, a bear, a serpent, a toad, than to a man in innocency. So that it is impossible to find sincerity in any soul till there is a work of grace wrought there by the Spirit of God; and hence it is that a man is but almost a Christian when he has done all.

Question 5

What is the reason that many go no further in the profession of religion than to be almost Christians?

REASON 1. It is because they deceive themselves in the truth of their own condition. They mistake their state and think it good and safe when it is bad and dangerous. A man may look upon himself as a member of Christ, and yet God may look upon him as a vessel of wrath, as a child of God, by looking more upon his sins than his graces, more upon his failings than his faith, more upon indwelling lusts than renewing grace, may think his case very bad when yet it is very good. "I am black," said the spouse; and yet said Christ, "O thou fairest among women!" So the sinner, by looking more upon his duties than his sins, may think he sees his name written in the Book of Life and yet be, in the account of God, a very reprobate.

There is nothing more common than for a man to think himself something when he is nothing, and so he deceives himself. Many a man blesses himself in his interest in Christ when he is indeed a stranger to Him. Many a man thinks his sin pardoned when, alas, he is still in the gall of bitterness, and bond of iniquity! Many a man thinks he has grace when he has none. "There is he," said Solomon, "that makes himself rich, and yet hath nothing." This was the very temper of Laodicea: "Thou sayest, I am rich and increased with goods, and have need of nothing; and knowest not (pray mind that) that thou art wretched, and miserable, and poor, and blind and naked."

"Thou knowest not." As bad as she was, she thought her state good. As poor as she was in grace, she thought she was rich. As miserable and naked as she was, yet she thought she had need of nothing.

FIVE GROUNDS FOR THIS MISTAKE

Now there are several rises or grounds of this mistake. I will name five to you.

1. *The desperate deceitfulness of the heart of every natural man.* "The heart is deceitful above all things." The Hebrew word is the same with Jacob's name. He was a supplanter of his brother Esau: "He rightly called Jacob," said he, "for he hath supplanted me these two times." So the word signifies to be fraudulent, subtle, deceitful, and supplanting. Thus, the heart of every natural man is "deceitful above all things."

You read of the deceitfulness of the tongue, the deceitfulness of riches, the deceitfulness of beauty, and of the deceitfulness of friends. Yet, the heart is deceitful above them all. Nay, you read of the deceitfulness of Satan. Yet, truly, a man's heart is a greater deceiver than he, for he could never deceive a man if his own heart did not deceive him. Now it is from hence that a man presumes upon the goodness of his case, from the desperate treachery of his own heart.

How common it is for men to boast of the goodness of their hearts! "I thank God, though I do not make such a show and pretence as some do, yet I have as good a heart as the best." O but hear Solomon in this case: "He that trusteth in his own heart is a fool." Will any wise man commit his money to the cut-purse? Will he trust a cheat? It is a good rule, "Remember to distrust"; and it was Austin's maxim, "That man that trusts his own heart shall be sure to find himself deceived at last."

2. *This mistake arises from the pride of a man's spirit.* There is a proud heart in every natural man. There was much of this pride in Adam's sin, and there is much of it in all Adam's sons. It is a radical sin, and from hence arises this overweening opinion of a man's state and condition. Solomon said, "Be not righteous overmuch." Austin, speaking occasionally of these words, said, "it is not meant of the righteousness of the wise man, but the pride of the presumptuous man." Now, in this sense, every carnal man is righteous overmuch; though he has none of that righteousness which commends him to God, to wit, the righteousness of Christ, yet he has too much of that righteousness which commends him to himself, and that is self-righteousness.

A proud man has an eye to see his beauty but not his deformity; his parts but not his spots; his seeming righteousness but not his real wretchedness. It must be a work of grace that must show a man the lack of grace. The haughty eye looks upward, but the humble eye looks downward; and, therefore, this is the believer's motto: "The least of saints, the greatest of sinners"; but the carnal man's motto is, "I thank God I am not as other men."

3. *Many deceive themselves with common grace instead of saving through that resemblance that is between them.* As many take counterfeit money for current coin, so too many take common grace for true. Saul took the devil

for Samuel because he appeared in the mantle of
Samuel; so many take common grace for saving,
because it is like saving grace, as man may be under a
supernatural work and yet fall short of a saving work.
The first raises nature, the second only renews nature.
Though every saving work of the Spirit is supernatural,
yet every supernatural work of the Spirit is not saving;
and hence many deceive their own souls by taking a
supernatural work for a saving work.

4. *Many mistake a profession of religion for a work of
conversion and outside reformation for a sure sign of inward
regeneration.* If the outside of the cup is washed, then
they think all is clean though it is never so foul within.
This is the common rock that so many souls split upon
to their eternal hazard, taking up a form of godliness
but denying the power thereof.

5. *Lack of a home application of the law of God to the
heart and conscience to reveal to a man the true state and
condition he is in.* Where this is lacking, a man will sit
down short of a true word of grace and will reckon his
case better than it is. That is a notable passage which
the apostle hints concerning himself: "I was alive without the law once; but when the commandment came,
sin revived, and I died." Here you have an account of
the different apprehensions Paul had of his condition
with and without the Word.

Here is his apprehension of his condition without
the Word. "I was alive," said he, "without the law." Paul
had the law, for he was a Pharisee; and they had the
"form of knowledge, and of the truth of the law."
Therefore, when he said he was without the law, you
must not take him literally but spiritually. He was without the power and efficacy of it upon his heart and

conscience convincing, awakening, and discovering sin. And, as long as this was his case, he did not doubt his state. He was confident of the goodness of his condition. This he hinted at when he said, "I was alive"; but then:

Here is his apprehension of his condition with the Word, and that is quite contrary to what it was before: "When the commandment came, said he, then sin revived, and I died." The Word of the Lord came with power upon his soul when the Spirit of God set it home effectually upon his conscience (that is meant by the coming of the commandment, "then sin revived, and I died"). That is, I saw the desperateness of my case and the filthiness of all my self-righteousness. Then my hope ceased and my confidence failed; and, as before I thought myself alive and my sin dead, so, when God had awakened conscience by the Word, then I saw my sin alive and powerful and myself dead and miserable. So that this is the first reason why men go no further in the profession of religion than to be almost Christians. It is because they mistake their state and think it is good when it is not; which mistake is fivefold:

1. A deceitful heart.
2. A proud spirit.
3. Taking common grace for saving.
4. Outward reformation for true regeneration.
5. Lack of home application of the law of God to the heart and conscience.

REASON 2. It is from Satan's cunning who, if he cannot keep sinners in their open profaneness, then he labors to persuade them to take up with a form of godliness. If he cannot entice them on in their lusts with a total neglect of heaven, then he entices them to such a profession as is sure to fall short of heaven. He will consent to the leaving of some sins as long as we keep the rest; to doing of some duties as long as we neglect the rest. Nay, rather than part with his interest in the soul, he will yield far to our profession of religion and consent to anything but our conversion and closing with Christ for salvation. He cares not which way we come to hell, as long as he gets us there at last.

REASON 3. It is from worldly and carnal policy. This is a great hindrance to many. Policy, many times, enters caveats against piety. Jehu will not part with his calves lest he hazard his kingdom. Among many men there would be more zeal and honesty were there less design and policy. There is an honest policy that helps religion, but carnal policy hinders it.

We are commanded to be wise as serpents. Now, the serpent is the subtlest of creatures; but, then, we must be as innocent as doves. If piety is without policy, it lacks security. If policy is without piety, it lacks integrity. Piety without policy is too simple to be safe, and policy without piety is too subtle to be good. Let men be as wise, as prudent, as subtle, as watchful as they will, but then let it be in the way of God. Let it be joined with holiness and integrity. That is a cursed wisdom that forbids a man to launch any further out in the depth of religion than he can see the land, lest he be taken in a storm before he can make safe to shore again.

REASON 4. There are some lusts espoused in the

heart that hinder a hearty closing with Christ. Though they bid fair, yet they do not come to God's terms. The young man would have eternal life, and he bid fair for it; a willing obedience to every command but one, but only one, and will not God abate him one? Is He so severe? Will He not come down a little in his terms when man rises so high? Must man yield all? Will God yield nothing? No, my brethren, he that underbids for heaven shall as surely lose it as he that will give nothing for it. He who will not give all he has, part with all for that "pearl of price", shall as surely go without it as he who never once cheapens it. Not coming up to God's terms is the ruin of thousands of souls. Nay, it is that upon which all who perish do perish. A naked sinner to a naked Christ, a bleeding broken sinner to a bleeding broken Christ: these are God's terms.

Most professors are like iron between two equal loadstones. God draws and they propend towards God; and the world draws and they incline to the world. They are between both. They would not leave God for the world if they might not be engaged to leave the world for God. But, if they must part with all, with every lust, every darling, every beloved sin, why, then, the spirit of Demas possesses them and God is forsaken by them.

My brethren, this is the great reason why many that are come to be almost Christians go no further. Some one beloved lust or other hinders them and, after long and high profession, parts them and Christ forever. They ran well, but here it is that they give out and, after all, fall short and perish to eternity.

Thus have I answered these five questions, namely:

1. How far may a man go in the way to heaven and

yet be but almost a Christian?

2. Why is it that a man is but almost a Christian when he has gone thus far?

3. What difference is there between this natural conscience in hypocrites and sinners and a renewed conscience in believers?

4. How is it that many are but almost Christians when they have gone thus far?

5. What is the reason that many go no further in the profession of religion than to be almost Christians?

Use of Application

INFERENCE 1. Salvation is not as easy a thing as it is imagined to be. This is attested by our Lord Jesus Christ Himself: "Strait is the gate, and narrow is the way that leadeth to life, and few there be that find it." The gate of conversion is a very difficult gate and yet every man who would be saved eternally must enter in at this strait gate, for salvation is impossible without it. "Except a man be born again," born from above, "he cannot see the kingdom of God."

Not that this gate is strait simply in respect of itself. No, for converting grace is free. The gate of mercy stands open all the day long. In the tenders of gospel grace, none are excluded unless they exclude themselves. Christ does not say, "If such and such will come to Me, I will not cast them out"; but "him that comes unto Me, be he who or what he will, if he has a heart to close with me, I will in no wise cast him out." He does not say, "If this or that man will, here is water for him"; but, "If any man will, let him take the water of life freely." Christ grudges mercy to none. Though salvation was dearly purchased for us, yet it is freely offered to us.

So that the gate which leads to life is not strait on Christ's part or in respect of itself, but it is strait in respect of us because our lusts and corruptions make the entrance difficult. A needle's eye is big enough for a thread to pass through, but it is a difficult passage for a cable rope. Either the needle's eye must be enlarged or the cable rope must be untwisted; otherwise, the entrance is impossible. So it is in this case - the gate of conversion is a very strait passage for a carnal corrupt sinner to go in. The soul can never pass through with any one lust beloved and espoused; and, therefore, the sinner must be untwisted from every lust. He must lay aside the love of every sin or he can never enter in at this gate, for it is a strait gate. And, when he is in at this strait gate, he meets with a narrow way to walk in. So our Lord Christ said, "Narrow is the way that leadeth to life"; and what way is this but the way of sanctification? "For without holiness no man shall ever see the Lord."

Now, this way of sanctification is a very narrow way, for it lies over the neck of every lust and in the exercise of every grace: subduing the one and improving the other; dying daily and yet living daily; dying to sin and living to God. This is the way of sanctification! Oh, how few are there that walk in this way! The broad way has many travellers in it, but this narrow way is like the ways of Canaan in the days of Shamgar. It is said, "In the days of Shamgar, the son of Anath, the highways were unoccupied, and the travellers walked through by-ways." In the Hebrew, it is, "through crooked ways;" the way of holiness is, by the most, an unoccupied way. So said the prophet. "A way shall be there, and it shall be called the way of holiness; the unclean shall not pass over it; no lion shall be there, nor any ravenous beasts shall go up thereon; but the redeemed shall walk there." The unclean, the lion, and the ravenous beast are in the crooked ways. None but the redeemed of the Lord walk in the way of the Lord.

It is no wonder, then, that our Lord Christ said of life that few there be that find it, when the gate is strait and the way narrow that leads to it. Many pretend to walk in the narrow way but they never entered in at the strait gate. Many pretend to have entered in at the strait gate but they walk not in the narrow way.

It is a very common thing for a man to perish upon a mistake of his way, to go on in those paths that take hold of hell and yet hope to find heaven at last. Those twenty paths forementioned run into destruction, yet many choose them and walk in them as the way of salvation. As many profane and open sinners perish by choosing the way of death, so many formal professors perish by mistaking the way of life. This I gather from what our Lord Christ said, "Few there be that find it"; which clearly implies what, in Luke 12:24, He plainly expresses; to wit, that many seek it. Many seek to enter in and yet are not able. Many run far and yet do not "so run as to obtain." Many bid fair for the pearl of price and yet go without it. Hell is had with ease but "the kingdom of heaven suffers violence."

INFERENCE 2. If many go thus far in the way to heaven and yet miscarry, oh, then, what shall be the end of those who fall short of these! If he shall perish who is almost a Christian, what shall he do who is not at *all* a Christian? If he that owns Christ, professes Christ, and leaves many sins for Christ may be damned notwithstanding; what, then, shall his doom be that disowns Christ and refuses to part with one sin, one lust, one oath for Christ; nay, who openly blasphemes the precious name of Christ! If he who is outwardly sanctified shall yet be eternally rejected, what will the case be of those who are openly unsanctified; who have not only the plague of a hard heart within, but also the plague-sore of a profane life without? If the formal professor must be shut out, surely the filthy adulterer, the swinish drunkard, the deep swearer, the profane Sabbath-breaker, the foul-mouthed scoffer, yea, and every carnal sinner much more. If there is a woe to him who falls short of heaven, then how sad is the woe to him who falls short of those who fall short of heaven? Ah, that God would make this an awakening word to sinners who are asleep in sin without the least fear of death or dread of damnation!

Use of Examination

Are there many in the world who are almost, and yet but almost, Christians? Why, then, it is time for us to call our condition into question and make a more narrow scrutiny into the truth of our spiritual estate; what it is, whether it is right or not; whether we are sound and sincere in our profession of religion or not. When our Lord Christ told His disciples, "One of you shall betray Me", every one began immediately to reflect upon himself. "Master, is it I? Master, is it I?" So should we do. When the Lord reveals to us from His Word how many there are under the profession of religion who are but almost Christians, we should straightway reflect upon our hearts, "Lord, is it I? Is my heart unsound? Am I but almost a Christian? Am I one of those who shall miscarry at last? Am I a hypocrite under a profession of religion? Have I form of godliness without the power?"

TWO QUESTIONS OF GREAT IMPORTANCE

There are two questions of very great importance which we should, every one of us, often put to ourselves: What am I? Where am I?

What am I? Am I a child of God or not? Am I sincere in religion or am I only a hypocrite under a profession?

Where am I? Am I yet in a natural state or a state of grace? Am I yet in the old root, in old Adam, or am I in the root, Christ Jesus? Am I in the covenant of works that ministers only wrath and death? Or am I in the covenant of grace that ministers life and peace?

Indeed, this is the first thing a man should look at. There must be a change of state before there can be a change of heart. We must come under a change of heart. We must come under a change of covenant before we can be under a change of condition, for the new heart and the new spirit is promised in the new covenant. There is nothing of that to be heard of in the old. Now, a man must be under the new covenant before he can receive the blessing promised in the new covenant. He must be in a new covenant state before he can receive a new covenant heart. No mercy, no pardon, no change, no conversion, no grace dispensed out of covenant. Therefore, this should be our great inquiry for, if we do not know where we are, we cannot know what we are; and if we know not what we are, we cannot be what we should be, namely, altogether Christians. Let me, then, I beseech you, press this duty upon you who are professors. Try your own hearts. "Examine yourselves whether you are in the faith; prove your own selves." I urge this upon most cogent arguments.

ARGUMENTS TO ENCOURAGE SELF-EXAMINATION

1. *Because many rest in a notion of godliness and outward shows of religion, yet remain in their natural condition.* Many are hearers of the Word but not doers of it,

and so deceive their own souls. Some neither hear nor do; these are profane sinners. Some both hear and do; these are true believers. Some hear but do not do; these are hypocritical professors.

He that slights the ordinances cannot be a true Christian; but yet it is possible a man may own them and profess them and yet be no true Christian. Whoever would trust a profession shall see Judas, a disciple, an apostle, a preacher of the gospel. He was one who cast out devils, yet cast out himself. "He is not a Jew who is one outwardly, neither is that circumcision which is outward in the flesh: but he is a Jew which is one inwardly; and circumcision is that of the heart, in the spirit, and not in the letter; whose praise is not of men, but of God."

2. *Because errors in the first foundation are very dangerous.* If we are not right in the main, in the fundamental work; if the foundation is not laid in grace in the heart, all our following profession comes to nothing. The house is built upon a sandy foundation and, though it may stand for while, yet, when the floods come and the winds blow and beat upon it, great will be the fall of it.

3. *Because many are the deceits that our souls are liable to in this case.* There are many things like grace that are not grace. Now, it is the likeness and similitude of things that deceive and make one thing to be taken for another. Many take gifts for grace, common knowledge for saving knowledge; whereas a man may have great gifts and yet no grace. He may have great knowledge and yet not know Jesus Christ.

Some take common faith for saving; whereas, a man may believe all the truths of the gospel, all the promises, all the threatenings, all the articles of the creed to be true, and yet perish for lack of saving grace.

Some take morality and restraining grace for piety and renewing grace; whereas it is common to have sin much restrained where the heart is not renewed.

Some are deceived with a half work, taking conviction for conversion, reformation for regeneration. We have many mermaid Christians; or, like Nebuchadnezzar's image, heads of gold and feet of clay. The devil cheats most men by a synecdoche, putting a part for the whole; partial obedience to some commands for universal obedience to all. Endless are the delusions that Satan fastens upon souls for lack of this self-search. It is necessary, therefore, that we try our state lest we take the shadow for the substance.

4. *Satan will try us at one time or other.* He will winnow us and sift us to the bottom; and, if we now rest in a groundless confidence, it will then end in a comfortless despair. Nay, God Himself will search and try us at the day of judgment especially, and who can abide that trial who never tries his own heart?

5. *Whatever a man's state is, whether he is altogether a Christian or not, whether his principles are sound or not, yet it is good to examine his own heart.* If he finds his heart good, his principles right and sound, this will be matter of rejoicing. If he finds his heart rotten, his principles false and unsound, the discovery is in order to a renewing. If a man has a disease upon him, and knows it, he may send to the physician in time; but what a sad vexation will it be not to see a disease till it is past cure? So, for a man to be graceless and not see it till it is too late, to think himself a Christian when he is not, and

that he is in the right way to heaven when he is in the ready way to hell, yet not know it till a death-bed or a judgment-day confutes his confidence - this is the most irrecoverable misery!

These are the grounds upon which I press this duty of examining our state. Oh, that God would help us in the doing this necessary duty!

QUESTION. You say, "But how shall I come to know whether I am almost or altogether a Christian? If a man may go so far and yet miscarry, how shall I know when my foundation is right, when I am a Christian indeed?"

ANSWER 1. The altogether Christian closes with and accepts Christ upon gospel terms. True union makes a true Christian. Many close with Christ but it is upon their own terms. They take and own Him but not as God offers Him. The terms upon which God in the gospel offers Christ are that we shall accept a broken Christ with a broken heart, a whole Christ with the whole heart - broken Christ with a broken heart as a witness of our humility, a whole Christ with a whole heart as a witness of our sincerity. A broken Christ respects His suffering for sin, a broken heart respects our sense of sin. A whole Christ includes all His offices, a whole heart includes all our faculties. Christ is a King, Priest, and Prophet, and all as a Mediator. Without any one of these offices, the work of salvation could not have been completed. As a Priest, He redeems us. As a Prophet, He instructs us. As a King, He sanctifies and saves us. Therefore, the apostle says, "He is made to us of God, wisdom, righteousness, sanctification, and redemption." Righteousness and redemption flow from

Him as a Priest; wisdom as a Prophet, sanctification as a King.

Now many embrace Christ as a Priest but they do not own Him as a King and Prophet. They like to share in His righteousness but not to partake of His holiness. They would be redeemed by Him but they would not submit to Him. They would be saved by His blood but not submit to His power. Many love the privileges of the gospel but not the duties of the gospel. Now, these are but almost Christians, notwithstanding their closing with Christ; for it is upon their own terms but not upon God's. The offices of Christ may be distinguished but they can never be divided. But the true Christian owns Christ in all His offices. He not only closes with Him as Jesus, but as *Lord* Jesus. He says with Thomas, "My Lord, and my God." He not only believes in the merit of His death but also conforms to the manner of His life. As he believes in Him, so he lives to Him. He takes Him for His wisdom as well as for His righteousness; for His sanctification as well as His redemption.

ANSWER 2. The altogether Christian has a thorough work of grace and sanctification wrought in the heart as a spring of duties. Regeneration is a whole change - "old things are done away and all things become new." It is a perfect work as to parts, though not as to degrees. Carnal men do duties but they are from an unsanctified heart, and that spoils all. A new piece of cloth never does well in an old garment, for the rent is but made worse. When a man's heart is thoroughly renewed by grace, the mind savingly enlightened, the conscience thoroughly convinced, the will truly humbled and subdued, the affections spiritually raised and sanctified; and when mind, will, conscience, and affections all join issue to help on with the performance of the duties commanded, then is a man altogether a Christian.

ANSWER 3. He who is altogether a Christian looks to the manner as well as to the matter of his duties; not only that they are done, but how they are done. He knows the Christian's privileges lie in pronouns, but his duty in adverbs; it must not only be *bonum*, good, but it must be *bene;* that good must be rightly done.

Here the almost Christian fails. He does the same duties that others do for the matter, but he does not do them in the same manner. While he minds the substance, he does not regard the circumstance. If he prays, he does not regard faith and fervency in prayer. If he hears, he does not mind Christ's rule, "Take heed how ye hear." If he obeys, he does not look to the frame of his heart in obeying and, therefore, miscarries in all he does. Any of these defects spoils the good of every duty.

ANSWER 4. The altogether Christian is known by his sincerity in all his performances. Whatever a man does in the duties of the gospel, he cannot be a Christian without sincerity. Now, the almost Christian fails in this; for, though he does much, prays much, hears much, and obeys much, he is a hypocrite under all.

ANSWER 5. He who is altogether a Christian has a correspondence within to the law without. There is a similarity between the Word of God and the will of a Christian. His heart is, as it were, the transcript of the Law. The same holiness that is commanded in His Word is implanted in the heart. The same conformity to Christ that is enjoined by the Word of God is wrought in the soul by the Spirit of God. The same obedience which the Word requires of him, the Lord enables him to perform by His grace bestowed on him. This is that which is promised in the new covenant: "I will put my law in their inward parts, and write it in their hearts." Now, writing His law in us is nothing else but His working that grace and holiness in us which the law commands and requires of us.

In the old covenant administration, God wrote His laws only upon tables of stone but not upon the heart; and, therefore, though God wrote them, yet they broke them. But, in the new covenant administration, God provides new tables (not tables of stone, but the fleshy tables of the heart) and writes His laws there that there might be a law within answerable to the law without. And this every true Christian has. So that he may say in his measure, as our Lord Christ did, "I delight to do Thy will, O my God; Thy law is within my heart." Every believer has a light within him, not guiding him to despise and slight but to prize and walk by the light without Him; for the Word commands him to walk in the light, and the light directs him to walk according to the Word. Moreover, from this impression of the law upon the heart, obedience and conformity to God becomes the choice and delight of the soul; for holiness is the very nature of the new creature so that, if there were no Scripture, no Bible to guide him, yet he would be holy, for he has received "grace for grace." There is a grace within to answer to the word of grace without. Now, the almost Christian is a stranger to this law of God within. He may have some conformity to the Word in outward conversation, but he cannot have this answerableness to the Word in inward constitution.

ANSWER 6. The altogether Christian is much in duty, and yet much above duty; much in duty in regard of performances, much above duty in regard of dependence; much in duty by obeying, but much above duty by believing. He lives in his obedience, not upon his obedience, rather upon Christ and His righteousness. The almost Christian fails in this. He is much in duty, but not above it. Rather he rests in it. He works for rest and he rests in his works. He cannot come to believe and obey too. If he believes, then he thinks there is no need of obedience and so casts off that. If he is much in obedience, then he casts off believing and thinks there is no need of that. He cannot say with David, "I have hoped for Thy salvation, and done Thy commandments." The more a man is in duty and the more above it, the more in doing and the more in believing, the more a Christian.

ANSWER 7. He who is altogether a Christian is universal in his obedience. He does not obey one command and neglect another, do one duty and cast off another, but he has respect to all the commands. He endeavors to leave every sin and love every duty.

The almost Christian fails in this. His obedience is partial and piece-meal. If he obeys one command, he breaks another. The duties that least cross his lust he is much in, but those that do he lays aside.

The Pharisees fasted, prayed, paid tithes, etc., but they did not lay aside their covetousness or their oppression. They devoured widows' houses, they were unnatural to parents.

ANSWER 8. The altogether Christian makes God's glory the chief end of all His performances. If he prays, hears, gives, fasts, repents, or obeys, etc., God's glory is the main end of all. It is true, he may have something else at the hither end of his work, but God is at the further end. As Moses's rod swallowed up the magicians' rods, so God's glory is the ultimate end that swallows up all his other ends. Now, the almost Christian fails in this. His ends are corrupt and selfish. God may possibly be at the one end of his work but self is at the other end, for he who was never truly cast out of himself can have no higher end than himself.

Now, then, examine yourself by these characters. Put the question to your own soul. Do you close with Christ upon gospel terms? Is grace in the heart the principle of your performances? Do you look to the manner as well as the matter of your duties? Do you do all in sincerity? Is there an answerableness within to the law without? Are you much above duty when much in duty? Is your obedience universal? Lastly, is God's glory the end of all? If so, then you are not only almost, but altogether a Christian.

Use of Caution

Oh, take heed of being almost, and yet but almost a Christian! It is a great complaint of God against Ephraim that "he is a cake not turned"; that is, half baked, neither raw nor roasted, neither cold nor hot, as Laodicea. "Because thou art neither cold nor hot, therefore I will spew thee out of My mouth." This is a condition that, of all others, is greatly unprofitable, exceedingly uncomfortable, and desperately dangerous.

It is greatly unprofitable to be but almost a Christian; for failing in any one point will ruin us as surely as if we had never made any attempts for heaven. It is no advantage to the soul to be almost converted, for the little that we lack spoils the good of all our attainments. We say, "as good never a whit as never the near." There is no profit in leaving this or that sin unless we leave all sin. Herod heard John gladly and did many things, but he kept his Herodias and that ruined him. Judas did many things - prayed much, preached much, professed much, but his covetousness spoiled all. One sin ruined the young man who had kept all the commands but one. Thus he who offends in one point is guilty of all. That is, he who lives wilfully and allowedly in any one sin brings the guilt of the violation of the whole law of God upon his soul, and that upon a twofold account:

1. Because he manifests the same contempt of the authority of God in the wilful breach of one as of all.

2. By allowing himself in the breach of any one

command, he shows he kept none in obedience and conscience to God; for he who hates sin as sin hates all sin, and he who obeys the command as the express will of God obeys every command. And, for this cause, the least sin, willfully and with allowance lived in, spoils the good of all our obedience and lays the soul under the whole wrath of God. One leak in a ship will sink her, though she is tight every way else. Gideon had seventy sons and but one bastard, and yet that one bastard destroyed all his sons. So may one sin spoil all our services. One lust beloved may spoil all our profession, as that one bastard slew all the sons of Gideon.

It is exceedingly uncomfortable, as appears four ways:

1. *In that such a one is hated of God and men.* The world hates him because of his profession and God abhors him because of his dissimulation. The world hates him because he seems good and God hates him because he only seems so. There is no person whom God hates more than the almost Christian. "I would that thou wert either cold or hot"; either all a Christian or not at all a Christian. "Because thou art neither cold nor hot, therefore I will spew thee out of my mouth." What a loathsome expression God here uses to show what an utter abhorrence there is in Him against lukewarm Christians! How uncomfortable, then, must that condition be where a man is abhorred both of God and man!

2. *It is uncomfortable in regard of sufferings.* Being almost a Christian will bring us into suffering; but being but almost a Christian will never carry us through suffering. In Matthew 13:20-21 it is said, "He that receiveth the seed into stony ground, the same is he that

hears the Word, and with joy receives it; yet hath he not root in himself, but dureth for a while; for when tribulation or persecution ariseth because of the Word, by and by he is offended."

There are four things observable in these words:

The stony ground may receive the word with joy.

It may, for some time, abide in a profession of it: "He dureth for a while."

This profession will expose to suffering; for mark, persecution is said to arise because of the Word.

This suffering will cause an apostatizing from profession, for that which is here called "offence" is, in Luke 8:13, called "falling away"; "which for a while believe, and in time of temptation fall away."

I gather hence that a profession may expose a man as much to suffering as the power of godliness; but, without the power of godliness, there is no holding out in a profession under suffering. The world hates the show of godliness and, therefore, persecutes it. The almost Christian lacks the substance and, therefore, cannot hold out in it.

Now this must be very uncomfortable. If I profess religion, I am likely to suffer; if I only profess it, I am never likely to endure.

3. *It is uncomfortable in regard of that deceit it lays our hopes under.* To be deceived of our hopes causes sorrow as well as shame. He that is but almost a Christian hopes for heaven; but, unless he is altogether a Christian, he shall never come there. Now, to perish with hopes of heaven; to go to hell by the gates of glory; to come to the very door and then be shut out (as the five virgins were); to die in the wilderness within the sight of the promised land at the very brink

of Jordan, this must be sad. To come within a stride of
the goal and yet miss it, to sink within sight of harbor,
oh, how uncomfortable is this!

4. *As it is greatly unprofitable, and exceedingly uncomfortable to be but almost a Christian, so it is desperately dangerous, for:*

This hinders the true work. A man lies in a fairer
capacity for conversion who lies in open enmity and
rebellion than he who soothes up himself in the for-
malities of religion. This I gather from the parable of
the two sons which our Lord Jesus Christ urged to the
professing Scribes and Pharisees. "There was a man
had two sons; and he came to one and said, Go to work
today in my vineyard. He said, I will not; but afterwards
repented and went. And he came to the second, and
said likewise; and he said, I go, Sir; but went not." The
first represents the carnal open sinner who is called by
the Word but refuses, yet afterwards repents and believes. The second represents the hypocritical professor who pretends much but performs little. Now, mark
how Christ applies this parable. "Verily I say unto you,
that the publicans and the harlot go into the kingdom
of God before you."

And, upon this account, it is better not to be at all
than to be almost a Christian, for the almost hinders
the all together. It is better, in this regard, to be a sinner without a profession than to be a professor without
conversion, for the one lies fairer for an inward change
while the other rests in an outward. Our Lord Christ
tells the Scribe, "Thou art not far from the kingdom of
God," yet never likely to come there. None further
from the kingdom of God than such as are not far
from the kingdom of God. As, for instance, where

there lies but one lust, one sin, between a soul and Christ, that soul is not far from Christ; but now, when the soul rests in this nearness to Christ and yet will not part with that one lust for Christ, but thinks his condition secured though that lust is not subdued, who is further from the kingdom of God than he? So our Lord Christ tells the young man, "One thing thou lackest." Why, he was very near heaven, near being a Christian altogether; he was very near being saved. He tells Christ he had kept all the commands. He lacked but one thing, I say, but one thing. But it was a great thing. That one thing he lacked was more than all things he had for it was the one thing necessary. It was a new heart, a work of grace in his soul, a change of state, a heart weaned from the world. This was the one thing, and he who lacks this one thing perishes with all his other things.

This condition is so like a state of grace that the mistake of it for grace is easy and common. It is very dangerous to mistake anything for grace that is not grace in that a man contents himself as if it were grace. Formality often dwells next door to sincerity and one sign serves both, and so the house may be easily mistaken and, by that means, a man may take up his lodging there and never find the way out again.

What one said of wisdom, "Many might have been wise had they not thought themselves so when they were otherwise", the same I may say of grace. Many a formal professor might have been a sincere believer had he not mistaken his profession for conversion, his duties for grace, and so rested in that for sincerity. That is but hypocrisy.

It is a degree of blasphemy to pretend to grace and

yet have no grace. I gather this from Revelation 2:9, "I know the blasphemy of them which say they are Jews, and are not." This place undergoes variety of constructions. Grotius and Paraeus do not make their blasphemy to lie in their saying they are Jews and are not, but to lie in the reproaches that these Jews fastened upon Christ, calling Him impostor, deceiver, one that had a devil, etc. Thomas Brightman goes another way and said, "This was the blasphemy of these Jews: they retained that way of worship that was abrogated, and thrust upon God those old rites and ceremonies which Jesus Christ had abolished and nailed to His cross, by which they overthrew the glory of Christ and denied His coming. But I conceive the blasphemy of these Jews to lie in this, that they said they were Jews and were not." A Jew here is not to be taken literally and strictly only, for one of the lineage of Abraham, but it is to be taken metonymically for a true believer, one of the spiritual seed of Abraham. "He is a Jew who is one inwardly"; so that for a man to say he is a Jew when he is not, to profess an interest in Christ when he has none, to say he has grace when he has none, this Christ calls blasphemy.

But why should Christ call this blasphemy? This is hypocrisy, but how may it be said to be blasphemy? Why, he blasphemes the great attribute of God's omniscience. He implicitly denies that God sees and knows our hearts and thoughts for, if a man believed the omnisciency of God, that He searches the heart and sees and knows all within, he would not dare to rest in a graceless profession of godliness. This, therefore, is blasphemy in the account of Christ.

THE DANGERS OF BEING AN ALMOST CHRISTIAN

1. *It is dangerous to be almost a Christian in that this stills and serves to quiet conscience.* Now, it is very dangerous to quiet conscience with anything but the blood of Christ. It is bad being at peace till Christ speak peace. Nothing can truly pacify conscience less than that which pacifies God, and that is the blood of the Lord Christ. Now the almost Christian quiets conscience but not with the blood of Christ. It is not a peace flowing from Christ's propitiation but a peace rising from a formal profession; not a peace of Christ's giving but a peace of his own making. He silences and bridles conscience with a form of godliness, and so makes it give way to an undoing, soul-destroying peace. He rocks it asleep in the cradle of duties and, then, it is a thousand to one it never awakens more till death or judgment.

Ah, my brethren, it is better to have conscience never quiet than quieted any way but by "the blood of sprinkling." A good conscience unquiet is the greatest affliction to saints, and an evil conscience quiet is the greatest judgment to sinners.

2. *It is dangerous to be almost a Christian in respect of the unpardonable sin, the sin that the Scripture said can never be forgiven, neither in this world nor in the world to come.* I mean the sin against the Holy Ghost. Now, only such are capable of sinning that sin as are but almost Christians. A true believer cannot; the work of grace in his heart, that seed of God which abides in him, secures him against it.

The profane, ignorant, open sinner cannot. Though he lives daily and hourly in sin, yet he cannot commit this sin for it must be from an enlightened mind. Every sinner, under the gospel especially, sins sadly against the Holy Ghost, against the strivings and motions of the Spirit. He resists the Holy Ghost, but yet this is not the sin against the Holy Ghost.

INGREDIENTS OF THE SIN AGAINST THE HOLY GHOST

There must be three ingredients to make up that sin.

First, it must be willful. "If we sin wilfully after we have received the knowledge of the truth, there remains no more sacrifice for sin."

Second, it must be against light and conviction, "after we have received the knowledge of the truth."

Third, it must be in resolved malice. Now, you shall find all these ingredients in the sin of the Pharisees, Matthew 12:22. Christ heals one who was "possessed with a devil"; a great work which all the people wondered at, verse 23. But what did the Pharisees say? See verse 24, "This fellow casteth out devils by the prince of devils." Now, that this was the sin against the Holy Ghost is clear for it was both wilful and malicious and against clear convictions. They could not but see that He was the Son of God and that this work was a peculiar work of the Spirit of God in Him. Yet they say, "He worked by the devil!" Whereupon Christ charged them with this sin against the Holy Ghost, verses 31-33 (compare this with Mark 3:28-30). Now, the Pharisees were a sort of great professors, whence I gather this conclusion - that it is the professor of religion that is the subject of this sin, not the open carnal sinner; not the true believer but the formal professor; not the sinner, for he has neither light nor grace; therefore, the formal professor, for he has light but no grace. Here, then, is the great danger of being almost a Christian - he is liable to this dreadful unpardonable sin.

Being but almost a Christian subjects us to apostasy. He who gets no good by walking in the ways of God will quickly leave them and walk no more in them. This I gather from Hosea 14:9. "Who is wise, and he shall understand these things? prudent, and he shall know them? for the ways of the Lord are right, and the just shall walk in them, but the transgressors shall fall therein."

"The just shall walk in them." He whose heart is renewed and made right with God shall keep close to God in his ways.

"But the transgressors shall fall therein." The word in the Hebrew is *peshangim*, from a word that signifies to prevaricate, so that we may read the words thus, "The ways of the Lord are right, and the just shall walk in them; but he that prevaricates (that is, a hypocrite) in the ways of God shall fall therein."

An unsound heart will never hold out long in the ways of God. "He was a burning and a shining light, and ye were willing for a season to rejoice in that light."

"For a season." For an hour, a short space, and then they left Him. It is a notable question Job puts concerning the hypocrite, "Will he delight himself in the Almighty? Will he always call upon God?"

He may do much, but these two things he cannot do:

He cannot make God his delight.

He cannot persevere in duties at all times and in all

conditions.

He will be an apostate at last. The scab of hypocrisy usually breaks out in the plague-sore of apostasy. Conversion ground is standing ground; it is *terra firma*; but a graceless profession of religion is a slippery and falling ground. Julian the apostate was first Julian the professor. I know it is possible that a believer may fall, yet he rises again, the everlasting arms are underneath. But, when the hypocrite falls, who shall help him up? Solomon said, "Woe to him that is alone when he falls!" that is, without interest in Christ. Why woe to him? "For he hath none to help him up." If Jesus Christ does not recover him, who can? David fell and was restored, for he had one to help him up; but Judas fell and perished, for he was alone.

3. *Being but almost a Christian provokes God to bring dreadful spiritual judgments upon a man.*

Barrenness is a spiritual judgment. Now, this provokes God to give us up to barrenness. When Christ found the fig tree that had leaves but no fruit, He pronounced the curse of barrenness upon it. "Never fruit grow on thee more." And so Ezekiel 47:11, "The miry places thereof, and the marshy places thereof, shall not be healed; they shall be given to salt."

A spirit of delusion is a sad judgment. Why, this is the judgment: he receives the truth, but not in the love of it. "Because they received not the love of the truth, that they might be saved; for this cause, God shall send them strong delusions."

To lose either light or sight, either ordinances or eyes, is a great spiritual judgment. Why, this is the almost Christian's judgment: he receives the truth but not in the love of it; "Because they received not the love of the truth, that they might be saved; for this cause, God shall send them strong delusions."

To lose either light or sight, either ordinances or eyes, is a great spiritual judgment. Why, this is the almost Christian's judgment: He who does not profit under the means provokes God to take away either light or sight; either the ordinances from before his eyes or else to blind his eyes under the ordinances.

To have a hard heart is a dreadful judgment, and there is no hypocrite but has a hard heart.

My brethren, it is a dreadful thing for God to give a man up to spiritual judgments! Now, this being almost a Christian provokes God to give a man up to spiritual judgments. Surely, therefore, it is a very dangerous thing to be almost a Christian.

4. *Being almost, and but almost, Christians will exceedingly aggravate our damnation.* The higher a man rises under the means, the lower he falls if he miscarries. He who falls but a little short of heaven will fall deepest into hell. He who has been nearest to conversion, being not converted, shall have the deepest damnation when he is judged. Capernaum's sentence shall exceed Sodom's for severity because she exceeded Sodom in the enjoyment of mercy. She received more from God, she knew more of God; she professed more for God, and yet was not right with God. Therefore, she shall be punished more by God. The higher the rise, the greater the fall. The higher the profession, the lower the damnation. He miscarries with a light in his hand. He perishes under many convictions, and convictions never end but in a sound conversion (as in all saints) or in a sad damnation (as in all hypocrites). Praying ground, hearing ground, professing ground, and con-

viction ground is of all the worst ground to perish upon.

Now then, to sum up all under this head.

If to be almost a Christian hinders the true work of conversion; if it is easily mistaken for conversion; if it is a degree of blasphemy; if this is that which quiets conscience; if this subjects a man to commit the unpardonable sin; if it lays us liable to apostasy; if it provokes God to give us up to spiritual judgments; and if it is that which exceedingly aggravates our damnation; surely, then, it is a very dangerous thing to be almost, and but almost, a Christian!

Oh, labor to be altogether Christians, to go further than they who have gone furthest and yet fall short! This is the great counsel of the Holy Ghost, "So run that ye may obtain. Give diligence to make your calling and election sure."

Use of Exhortation

Do you need any motives to quicken you up to this important duty?

CONSIDERATION 1. This is that which is not only commanded by God, but that whereunto all the commands of God tend. A perfect conformity of heart and life to God is the sum and substance of all the commands both of the Old and the New Testament. As the harlot was for the dividing of the child, so Satan is for dividing the heart. He would have our love and affections shared between Christ and our lusts, for he knows that Christ reckons that we do not love Him at all unless we love Him above all. But God will have all or none: "My son, give my thy heart. Thou shalt love the Lord thy God with all thy heart, with all thy soul, and with all thy might." Look into the Scripture and see what that is upon which your "only" stands, and you shall find that God has fixed it upon those great duties which alone tend to the perfection of your state as Christians. God has fixed your "only" upon believing: "only believe." God has fixed your only upon obedience: "Thou shalt worship the Lord thy God, and Him only shalt thou serve. Only let your conversation be such as becometh the gospel of Christ." So that your "only" is fixed by God upon these two great duties of believing and obeying, both which tend to the perfection of your state as Christians.

Now, shall God command and shall we not obey? Can there be a higher motive to duty than the authority of the great God whose will is the eternal rule of righteousness? Oh, let us fear God and keep His commandments, for this is the whole of man!

CONSIDERATION 2. The Lord Christ is a Saviour throughout, a perfect and complete Mediator. He has not shed his blood by halves, nor satisfied the justice of God and redeemed sinners by halves. No! He went through with His undertaking. He bore all our sins and shed all His blood. He died to the utmost, satisfied the justice of God to the utmost, redeemed sinners to the utmost and, now that He is in heaven, He intercedes to the utmost and is able to save to the utmost.

It is observed that our Lord Christ, when He was upon the earth in the days of His flesh, wrought no half-cures; but whomever they brought to Him for healing He healed them throughout: "They brought unto him all that were diseased, and besought Him that they might only touch the hem of His garment, and as many as touched were made perfectly whole."

Oh, what an excellent Physician is here! None like Him! He cures infallibly, suddenly, and perfectly!

He cures infallibly. None ever came to Him for healing that went without it. He never practiced upon any who miscarried under His hand.

He cures suddenly. No sooner is His garment touched but His patient is healed. The leper, Matthew 8:3, is no sooner touched but immediately cured. The two blind men, Matthew 20:34, are no sooner touched but their eyes were immediately opened.

He cures perfectly. "As many as were touched, were made perfectly whole."

Now, all this was to show what a perfect and complete Saviour Jesus Christ would be to all sinners who would come to Him. They should find healing in His blood, virtue in His righteousness, and pardon for all their sins, whatever they were. Look, as Christ healed all the diseases of all who came to Him when He was on earth, so He pardons all the sins and heals all the wounds of all those souls that come to Him now that He is in heaven! He is a Saviour throughout and shall not we be saints throughout? Shall He be altogether a Redeemer and shall we not be altogether believers? Oh, what a shame is this!

CONSIDERATION 3. There is enough in religion to engage us to be altogether Christians; and that whether we respect profit or comfort, for grace brings both.

First, religion is a gainful thing; and this is a compelling motive that becomes effectual upon all. Gain is the god whom the world worships. What will not men do, what will they not suffer, for gain? What journeys men take by land, what voyages by sea, through hot and cold, through fair and foul, through storm and shine, through day and night, and all for gain! Now, there is no calling so gainful as this of religion. It is the most profitable employment we can take up. "Godliness is profitable unto all things." It is a great revenue. If it is closely followed, it brings in the greatest income. Indeed, some men are religious for the world's sake; such shall be sure not to gain, but they who are religious for religion's sake shall be sure not to lose if heaven and earth can recompense them; for "godliness hath the promise both of the life that now is, and of that which is to come."

Ah, who would not be a Christian when the gain of godliness is so great! Many gain much in their worldly calling, but the profit which the true believer has from one hour's communion with God in Christ weighs down all the gain of the world. "Cursed be the man who counts all the gain of the world worth one hour's communion with Jesus Christ," said that noble marquis, Galeacius Caracciola. It is nowhere said in Scripture, "Happy is the man who finds silver and the man that gets gold." These are of no weight in the balance of the sanctuary; but it is said, "Happy is the man that findeth wisdom, and the man that getteth understanding; for the merchandise of it is better than the merchandise of silver, and the gain thereof than fine gold." By wisdom and understanding here, we are to understand the grace of Christ, and so the Spirit of God interprets it. "Behold the fear of the Lord, that is wisdom; and to depart from evil is understanding." Now, of all merchants, he who trades in this wisdom and understanding will prove the richest man. One grain of godliness outweighs all the gold of Ophir.

THE UNIQUENESS OF THE RICHES OF GRACE

There are no riches like being rich in grace; for:

1. *These are the most necessary riches; other things are not so.* Silver and gold are not so, we may be happy without them. There is but one thing necessary and that is the grace of Jesus Christ in the heart. Have this and have all; lack this and want all.

2. *It is the most substantial gain.* The things of this world are more shadow than substance. Pleasure,

honor, and profit comprehend all things in this world
and, therefore, are the carnal man's trinity. The apostle John calls them "the lust of the flesh, the lust of the
eyes, and the pride of life;" this (said he) is all that is in
the world. And, truly, if this is all, all is nothing; for
what is pleasure but a dream and conceit? What is
honor but fancy and opinion? And what is profit but a
thing of nought? "Why wilt thou set thine eyes upon
that which is not?" The things of the world have in
them no sound substance, though foolish carnal men
call them substance. But, now, grace is a substantial
good; so our Lord Christ calls it. "That I may cause
those that love Me to inherit substance", to inherit that
which is. Grace is a reality; other things are but show
and fancy.

3. *Godliness is the safest gain.* The gain of worldly
things is always with difficulty but seldom with safety.
The soul is often hazarded in the over-eager pursuit of
worldly things. Nay, thousands pawn, lose, and damn
their precious souls eternally for a little silver and gold,
which are but the dross and garbage of the earth. And
"what is a man profited to gain the whole world if he
loses his own soul?" But the gain of godliness is ever
with safety to the soul. Nay, the soul is lost and undone
without it and not saved but by the attainment of it. A
soul without grace is in a lost and perishing condition;
the hazard of eternity is never over with us until the
grace of Christ Jesus is sought by us and wrought in us.

4. *Godliness is the surest profit.* As it is safe, so it is
sure. Men make great ventures for the world, but all
runs upon uncertainty. Many venture much and wait
long and yet find no return but disappointment. They
sow much and yet reap nothing. But the gain of godli-

ness is sure; "to him that soweth righteousness shall be a sure reward."

As the things of this world are uncertain in the getting, so they are uncertain in the keeping. If men do not undo us, moths may. If robbery does not, rust may. If rust does not, fire may; to which all earthly treasures are incident, as our Lord Christ teaches us, Matthew 6:19. Solomon paints the world with wings: "Riches make themselves wings, and fly as an eagle towards heaven." A man may be as rich as Dives today and yet poor as Lazarus tomorrow. Oh, how uncertain are all worldly things! But, now, the true treasure of grace is in the heart; that can never be lost. It is out of the reach both of rust and robber. He who gets the world gets a good he can never keep, but he who gets grace gets a good he shall never lose.

5. *The profit of godliness lies not only in this world but in the world to come.* All other profit lies in this world only; riches and honour, etc., are called this world's goods, but the riches of godliness are chiefly in the other world's goods; in the enjoyment of God, Jesus Christ, and the Holy Spirit among saints and angels in glory. Lo, this is the gain of godliness. Such honor have all His saints.

6. *The gain of godliness is a durable and eternal gain.* All this world's goods are perishing - perishing pleasures, perishing honors, perishing profits, and perishing comforts. "Riches are not forever," said Job. "Hast thou entered into the treasures of the snow?" Gregory, upon these words, observed that earthly treasures are treasures of snow. What pains children take to scrape and roll the snow together to make a snowball, which is no sooner done but the heat of the sun dissolves it and

it comes to nothing! Why, the treasures of worldly men are but treasures of snow. When death and judgment come, they melt away and come to nothing. "Riches profit not in the day of wrath, but righteousness delivers from death."

You see here the great advantage of godliness; so that, if we look at profit, we shall find enough in religion to engage us to be altogether Christians.

Second, if we look at comfort, religion is the most comfortable profession. There are no comforts to be compared to the comforts of grace and godliness.

MARKS OF WORLDLY COMFORT

Worldly comfort is only outward. It is but skin deep. In the midst of laughter, the heart is sorrowful. But, now, the comfort that flows from godliness is an inward comfort, a spiritual joy; therefore, it is called gladness of heart. "Thou hast put gladness in my heart." Other joys smooth the brow but this fills the breast.

Worldly comfort has a nether spring. The spring of worldly comfort is in the creature in some earthly enjoyment; and, therefore, the comfort of worldly men must be mixed and muddy. An unclean fountain cannot send forth pure water, but spiritual comfort has an upper spring. The comfort that accompanies godliness flows from the manifestations of the love of God in Christ, from the workings of the blessed Spirit in the heart, which is first a counsellor and then a comforter; and, therefore, the comforts of the saints must be pure and unmixed comforts for they flow from a pure spring.

Worldly comfort is very fading and transitory. "The triumphing of the wicked is but short, and the joy of the hypocrite is but for a moment." Solomon compares it to the "crackling of thorns under a pot", which is but a blaze and soon out. So is the comfort of carnal hearts.

MARKS OF GODLY COMFORT

But, now, the comfort of godliness is a durable and abiding comfort. Your heart shall rejoice, and your joy no man shall take from you. The comfort of godliness is lasting and everlasting. It abides by us in life, in death, and after death.

1. *First, it abides by us in life.* Grace and peace go together. Godliness naturally brings forth comfort and peace. The effect of righteousness shall be peace. It is said of the primitive Christians, "They walked in the fear of the Lord and in the comfort of the Holy Ghost." Every duty done in uprightness and sincerity reflects some comfort upon the soul. "In keeping Thy commands, there is a great reward;" not only *for* keeping them, but *in* keeping them. As every flower, so every duty, carries sweetness and refreshing with it.

OBJECTION. But who is more dejected and disconsolate than saints and believers? Whose lives are more uncomfortable? Whose mouths are more filled with complaints than theirs? If a condition of godliness and Christianity is a condition of so much comfort, then why are they thus?

SOLUTION. That the people of God are often-times without comfort, I grant. They may walk in the dark and have no light, but this is none of the products of godliness. Grace brings forth no such fruit as this.

WHY SAINTS ARE SOMETIMES WITHOUT COMFORT

There is a threefold rinse and spring of it: sin within, desertions, and temptation without.

1. *Sin within.* The saints of God are not all spirit and no flesh, all grace and no sin. They are made up of contrary principles. There is light and darkness in the same mind, sin and grace in the same will, carnal and spiritual in the same affections. There is "the flesh lust-ing against the spirit." In all these, and too often, the Lord knows, the believer is led away captive by these warring lusts. So was the holy apostle himself: "I find then a law that, when I would do good, evil is present with me. I see another law in my members, warring against the law of my mind, and bringing me into cap-tivity to the law of sin;" and this was that which broke his spiritual peace and filled his soul with trouble and complaints, as you see: "O wretched man that I am! who shall deliver me from this body of death?" So that it is sin that interrupts the peace of God's people. Indwelling lust, stirring and breaking forth, must cause trouble and grief in the soul of a believer; for it is as natural for sin to bring forth trouble as it is for grace to bring forth peace. Every sin contracts a new guilt upon the soul, and guilt provokes God; and, where there is a sense of guilt contracted and God provoked, there can be no peace and no quiet in the soul till faith procures

fresh sprinklings of the blood of Jesus Christ upon the conscience.

2. *Another spring of the believer's trouble and disconsolateness of spirit is the desertions of God, and this follows upon the former.* God sometimes disappears and hides Himself from His people: "Verily, Thou art a God that hidest Thyself." But the cause of God's hiding is the believer's sinning: "Your iniquities have separated between you and your God, and your sins have hid His face from you." In heaven, where there is no sinning, there is no losing the light of God's countenance for a moment; and, if saints here could serve God without corruption, they should enjoy God without desertion. But this cannot be. While we are in this state, remaining lusts will stir and break forth and, then, God will hide His face. This must be trouble. "Thou didst hide Thy face, and I was troubled."

The light of God's countenance shining upon the soul is the Christian's heaven on this side of heaven; and, therefore, it is no wonder if the hiding of His face is looked upon by the soul as one of the days of hell. So it was by David: "The sorrows of death compassed me, the pains of hell gat hold upon me; I found trouble and sorrow."

3. *A third spring of that trouble and complaint that brims the banks of the Christian's spirit is the temptations of Satan.* He is the great enemy of saints, and he envies the quiet and comfort that their hearts are filled with when his conscience is brimmed with horror and terror. Therefore, though he knows that he cannot destroy their peace, still he labors to disturb their peace. As the blessed Spirit of God is first a Sanctifier and then a Comforter, working grace in order to peace, so this

cursed spirit of hell is first a tempter and then a troubler; first persuading to act sin and then accusing for sin. This is his constant practice upon the spirits of God's people. He cannot endure that they should live in the light of God's countenance when himself is doomed to eternal, intolerable darkness.

And thus you see why it is that the people of God are often under trouble and complaint. All arises from these three springs of sin within, desertions and temptations without.

If the saints could serve God without sinning, and enjoy God without yielding, they might enjoy peace and comfort without sorrowing. This must be endeavored constantly here, but it will never be attained fully but in heaven. But yet, so far as grace is the prevailing principle in the heart, and so far as the power of godliness is exercised in this life, so far the condition of a child of God is a condition of peace; for it is an undoubted truth that the fruit of righteousness shall be peace. But suppose the people of God experience little of this comfort in this life; yet:

They find it in the day of death. Grace and holiness will minister unto us then and that ministration will be peace. A believer has a twofold spring of comfort, each one emptying itself into his soul in a dying season. One is from above him, the other is from within him. The spring that runs comfort from above him is the blood of Christ sprinkled upon the conscience. The spring that runs comfort from within him is the sincerity of his heart in God's service. When we lie upon a deathbed and can reflect upon our principles and performances in the service of God, and there find uprightness and sincerity of heart running through all, this must be comfort. It was so to Hezekiah: "Remember, O Lord, how I have walked before Thee in truth, and with a perfect heart; and have done that which is good in Thy sight."

Nothing makes a deathbed so uneasy and hard as a life spent in the service of sin and lust; nothing makes a deathbed so soft and sweet as a life spent in the service of God and Christ. Or put the case, the people of God should not meet with this comfort then; yet,

They shall be sure to find it after death. If time brings none of this fruit to ripeness, yet eternity shall. Grace in time will be glory in eternity; holiness now will be happiness then. "Whatever it is a man soweth in this world, that he shall be sure to reap in the next world; he that soweth to the flesh, shall of the flesh reap corruption; but he that soweth to the spirit shall of the spirit reap life everlasting." When sin shall end in sorrow and misery, holiness shall end in joy and glory: "Well done, thou good and faithful servant, enter thou into the joy of thy Lord." Whoever shares in the grace of Christ in this world shall share in the joys of Christ in the world to come, and that joy is joy unspeakable and full of glory. Lo, here is the fruit of godliness. See now if there is not enough in religion, whether we respect profit or comfort, to engage us to be Christians throughout.

CONSIDERATION 4. What an entire resignation wicked men make of themselves to their lusts! And shall not we do so to the Lord Christ? They give up themselves without reserve to the pleasures of sin, and shall we have our reserves in the service of God? They are altogether sinners, and shall not we be altogether saints? They run and faint not in the service of their lusts, and shall we faint and not run in the service of Christ? Shall the servants of corruption have their ears bored to the doorposts of sin in token of an entire and perpetual service, and shall we not give up ourselves to the Lord Christ to be His forever? Shall others make a covenant with hell and death, and shall we not join ourselves to God in an everlasting covenant that cannot be forgotten? Shall they take more pains to damn their souls than we do to save ours? Shall they make more speed to a place of vengeance than we do to a crown of righteousness? Which do you judge best, to be saved everlastingly or to perish everlastingly? Which do you count the best master, God or the devil? Christ or your lusts? I know you will determine it on Christ's side. Oh, then, when others serve their lusts with all their hearts, you serve Christ with all your hearts! If the hearts of the sons of men are fully set in them to do evil, then, much more, let the hearts of the sons of God be fully set in them to do good.

CONSIDERATION 5. If you are not altogether Christians, you will never be able to appear with comfort before God, nor to stand in the judgment of the last and great day. For this sad dilemma will silence every hypocrite: "If My commands were not holy, just, and good, why did you not own them? If they were holy, just, and good, why did you not obey them? If Jesus Christ was not worth having, why did you profess Him? If He was, then why did you not cleave to Him and close with Him? If My ordinances were not appointed to convert and save souls, why did you sit under them and rest in the performance of them? Or, if

they were, then why did you not submit to the power in
them? If religion is not good, why do you profess it? If
religion is good, why do you not practice it? 'Friend,
how did you come in here, not having a wedding
garment?' If it was not a wedding feast, why did you
come at the invitation? If it was, then why did you
come without a wedding garment?"

I would but ask a hypocritical professor of the
gospel what he will answer in that day. Verily, you de-
prive yourselves of all possibility of apology in the day
of the righteous judgment of God. It is said of the man
who had no wedding-garment on that, when Christ
came and examined him, he was speechless. He who is
graceless in a day of grace will be speechless in a day of
judgment. Professing Christ, without a heart to close
with Christ, will leave our souls inexcusable and make
our damnation unavoidable and more intolerable.

These are the motives to enforce the duty and, oh,
that God would set them home upon your hearts and
consciences that you might not dare to rest a moment
longer in a halfwork, or in being Christians within a little, but that you might be altogether Christians!

QUESTION. But you will say possibly, "How shall I
do it? What means shall I use that I may attain to a
thorough work in my heart that I may be no longer
almost, but altogether a Christian?"

ANSWER. Now I shall lay down three rules of direction instead of many to further and help you in this
important duty, and so leave this work to God's blessing.

Direction 1. Break off all false peace of conscience.
This is the devil's bond to hold the soul from seeking

after Christ. As there is the peace of God, so there is
the peace of Satan; but they are easily known for they
are as contrary as heaven and hell, as light and darkness. The peace of God flows from a work of grace in
the soul and is the peace of a regenerate state; but the
peace of Satan is the peace of an unregenerate state. It
is the peace of death. In the grave, Job said, there is
peace: "There the wicked cease from troubling"; so a
soul dead to sin is full of peace; the wicked one troubles him not. The peace of God in the soul is a peace
flowing from removal of guilt by justifying grace:
"Being justified by faith in His blood, we have peace
with God"; but the peace of Satan in the soul arises and
is maintained by a stupidity of spirit and insensibility of
guilt upon the conscience. The peace of God is a peace
from sin that fortifies the heart against it: "The peace
of God that passeth all men's understanding, shall
keep your hearts and minds through Christ Jesus." The
more of this peace there is in the soul, the more is the
soul fortified against sin; but the peace of Satan is
peace *in* sin: "The strong man armed keeps the house,
and there is all at peace."

The saint's peace is a peace with God but not with
sin. The sinner's peace is a peace with sin but not with
God. And this is a peace better broken than kept. It is a
false, a dangerous, and an undoing peace. My brethren, death and judgment will break all peace of conscience, but not that which is wrought by Christ in the
soul and is the fruit of the "blood of sprinkling."
"When He gives quietness, who can make trouble?"
Now the peace that death will break, why should you
keep? Who would be fond of that quietness which the
flames of hell will burn in sunder? And yet how many

travel to hell through the fool's paradise of a false peace! Oh, break off this peace! For we can have no peace with God in Christ while this peace remains in our hearts. The Lord Christ gives no peace to them who will not seek it; and that man will never seek it who does not see his need of it; and he who is at peace in his lusts sees no need of the peace of Christ. The sinner must be wounded for sin, and troubled under it, before Christ will heal his wounds and give him peace from it.

Direction 2. Labor after a thorough work of conviction. Every conviction will not do. The almost Christian has his convictions as well as the true Christian or else he would have never gone so far; but they are not sound and right convictions or else he would have gone further. God will have the soul truly sensible of the bitterness of sin before it shall taste the sweetness of mercy. The plow of conviction must go deep and make deep furrows in the heart before God will sow the precious seed of grace and comfort there so that it may have depth of earth to grow in. This is the constant method of God - first to show man his sin, then his Saviour; first his danger, then his Redeemer; first his wound, then his cure; first his own vileness, then Christ's righteousness. We must be brought to cry out, "Unclean, unclean!" to mourn for Him whom we have pierced and, then, He sets open for us a fountain to wash in for sin and uncleanness. That is a notable place, Job 33:27-28, "He looked upon men; and if any say, I have sinned, and perverted that which was right, and it profited me not; he will deliver his soul from going into the pit, and his life shall see the light." The sinner must see the unprofitableness of his unrighteousness before he profits by Christ's righteousness. The Israelites are first stung with the fiery serpents and then the brazen serpent is set up. Ephraim is first thoroughly convinced and then God's bowels of mercy work toward him. Thus it was with Paul, Manasseh, the jailor, etc. So that this is the unchangeable method of God in working grace - to begin with conviction of sin. Oh, therefore, labor for thorough conviction!

Three Things We Must be Convinced of

And there are three things we should especially be convinced of:

1. *Be convinced of the evil of sin, the filthy and heinous nature of it.* This is the greatest evil in the world. It wrongs God, it wounds Christ, it grieves the Holy Spirit, and it ruins a precious soul. All other evils are not to be named with this. My brethren, though to do sin is the worst work, yet to see sin is the best sight; for sin discovered in its vileness makes Christ to be desired in His fulness. But above all, labor to be convinced of the mischief of an unsound heart. What an abhorrence it is to God, what certain ruin it brings upon the soul! Oh, think often upon the hypocrite's hell! "For this people's heart is waxed gross, and their ears are dull of hearing, and their eyes they have closed; lest at any time they should see with their eyes, and hear with their ears, and should understand with their heart, and should be converted, and I should heal them."

2. *Be convinced of the misery and desperate danger of a natural condition;* for, till we see the plague of our hearts and the misery of our state by nature, we shall never be brought off ourselves to seek help in another.

3. *Be convinced of the utter insufficiency and inability of anything below Christ Jesus to minister relief to your soul in this case.* All things besides Jesus Christ are physicians of no value. Duties, performances, prayers, tears, and self-righteousness avail nothing in this case. They make us like the troops of Tema, to return ashamed at our disappointment from such failing brooks.

Alas! It is an infinite righteousness that must satisfy for us, for it is an infinite God that is offended by us. If ever your sin is pardoned, it is infinite mercy that must pardon it. If ever you are reconciled to God, it is infinite merit must do it. If ever your heart is changed and your state renewed, it is infinite power must effect it; and if ever your soul escapes hell and is saved at last, it is infinite grace must save it.

In these three things right and sound conviction lies; and, wherever the Spirit of God works these thorough convictions, it is in order to a true and sound conversion; for, by this means, the soul is brought under a right qualification for the receiving of Christ.

You must know that a sinner can never come to Christ, for he is dead in sin, in enmity against Christ, an enemy to God and the grace of God; but there are certain qualifications that come between the soul's dead state in sin and the work of conversion and closing with Christ whereby the soul is put into a capacity of receiving the Lord Jesus Christ; for no man is brought immediately out of his dead state and made to believe in Jesus Christ. There are some qualifications coming in between. Now, sound convictions are the right qualifications for the sinner's receiving Christ; for He "came not to call the righteous, but sinners to repentance"; that is, such as see themselves sinners and, thereby, in a lost condition. So Luke exemplifies it: "The Son of man is come to seek and to save that which was lost. He is anointed, and sent to bind up the broken-hearted, to comfort all that mourn."

Oh, therefore, if you would be sound Christians, get sound convictions! Ask those who are believers indeed, and they will tell you that, had it not been for their convictions, they would never have sought after Christ for sanctification and salvation. They will tell you that they would have perished if they had not perished; they would have been in eternal bondage but for their spiritual bondage, had they not been lost as to Christ.

Direction 3. Never rest in convictions till they end in conversion. This is that wherein most men miscarry. They rest in their convictions and take them for conversion, as if sin seen were therefore forgiven, or as if a sight of the lack of grace were the truth of the work of grace.

You who are at any time under convictions, oh, take heed of resting in them! Though it is true that conviction is the first step to conversion, yet it is not conversion. A man may carry his convictions along with him into hell.

What is it that troubles poor creatures when they come to die but this: "I have not improved my convictions. At such a time I was convinced of sin, but yet I still went on in sin in the face of my convictions. In such a sermon I was convinced of such a duty, but I slighted the conviction; I was convinced of my lack of Christ, and of the readiness of Christ to pardon and save, but alas! I did not follow the conviction."

My brethren, remember this: slighted convictions

are the worst deathbed companions. There are two things especially which, above all others, make a deathbed very uncomfortable: purposes and promises not performed; and convictions slighted and not improved.

When a man takes up purposes to close with Christ, and yet puts them not into execution; and when he is convinced of sin and duty and yet does not improve his convictions, oh, this will sting and wound at last!

Now, therefore, has the Spirit of the Lord been at work in your souls? Have you ever been convinced of the evil of sin, of the misery of a natural state, of the insufficiency of all things under heaven to help, of the fulness and righteousness of Jesus Christ, of the necessity of resting upon Him for pardon and peace, and for sanctification and salvation? Have you ever been really convinced of these things? Oh, then, as you love your own souls, as ever you hope to be saved at last and enjoy God forever, improve these convictions and be sure you do not rest in them till they rise up to a thorough closing with the Lord Jesus Christ, and so end in a sound and perfect conversion! Thus shall you be not only almost, but altogether a Christian.

THE END